RECONCILIATION

The Boston Theological Institute Series

The Boston Theological Institute Series
Volume 3

RECONCILIATION

Mission and Ministry
in a Changing Social Order

Robert J. Schreiter, C.PP.S.

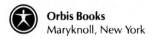
Orbis Books
Maryknoll, New York

Boston Theological Institute
Cambridge, Massachusetts

Ninth Printing, November 2002

The Catholic Foreign Mission Society of America (Maryknoll) recruits
and trains people for overseas missionary service. Through Orbis Books,
Maryknoll aims to foster the international dialogue that is essential to
mission. The books published, however, reflect the opinions of their
authors and are not meant to represent the official position of the society.

Copyright © 1992 by Robert J. Schreiter
Published by Orbis Books, Maryknoll, New York 10545 and
Boston Theological Institute, Newton, Massachusetts 02159
Printed in the United States of America

Scripture quotations are from the New Revised Standard Version of the
Bible copyrighted © 1989, Division of Christian Education of the
National Council of Churches of Christ in the United States of America,
and are used with permission.

Library of Congress Cataloging-in-Publication Data

Schreiter, Robert J.
    Reconciliation : mission and ministry in a changing social order /
Robert J. Schreiter.
        p.   cm. — (The Boston Theological Institute series ; v. 3)
    Includes bibliographical references.
    ISBN 0-88344-809-2
    1. Reconciliation — Religious aspects — Christianity.   2. Violence —
Religious aspects — Christianity.   3. Reconciliation — Biblical
teaching.   I. Title.   II. Series
BT736.15.S34   1992
234'.5 — dc20   91-40877
                                                                           CIP

Contents

Foreword

As Robert Schreiter surveys a sample of the political contexts around us that call for reconciliation, he refuses to take us down paths of appeasement—a hasty peace that trivializes physical or psychic violence, pacification without human liberation from structures that enslave, or mere conciliation through conflict management. Schreiter's perspective on the effects of violence, and thus the depths at which reconciliation must heal, runs deeper. The most insidious aspect of violence, or victimization, he shows, is the way in which it undoes our most basic physical and psychic safety and selfhood and which is reflected in the resultant false narratives that purport to give our lives meaning.

Oppressors, in Schreiter's reading of situations of violence, distort reality as another story, a "narrative of the lie," which is put forward to enfold their victims in another's—the violent one's—reality. This lie can only be overcome by a stronger, redeeming narrative. To develop such a narrative, Schreiter argues, pushes us beyond orthodoxy and orthopraxy to an orthopathema, a right way of suffering, that enables us to regain our humanity.

The writings of Paul provide Schreiter with the lens by which to understand Christian reconciliation and the Gospel as the stronger narrative. Through images of death, blood, and cross (reminding us of his earlier book *In Water*

and in Blood: A Spirituality of Solidarity and Hope
[1988]), Schreiter helps us to see Christian reconciliation
as rooted in three different theological realities: christological, ecclesiastical, and cosmic. Grounded as such, reconciliation is, finally, a spirituality or mode of being more
than a strategy. It comes upon us like healing.

Can the church participate in the ministry of reconciliation? For Christians the question is, perhaps, too quickly
answered in the affirmative. The legitimacy of Christianity, as we know only too well, is and often has been com-
promised by its silence and complicity with victimizers in
the interest of *Realpolitik*. Thus all the more intriguing
are Schreiter's remarks about the reality (perhaps prophetic necessity) for communities of Christians to distance
themselves (for a while) from the larger church in their
search for and discovery of reconciliation—particularly if
that larger church is implicated in the very violence it
seeks to overcome. Here might be found the germinal
ideas of what could be called a psychological history of
organizations—or what an earlier generation referred to
as the spiritual history of the church. Again, the question:
Can the church (as concrete congregations of Christians!)
participate in the ministry of reconciliation? With an
appropriate sense of its (and our) own sin and limitations,
Schreiter's answer is in the affirmative.

This answer is given without any triumphalism. In fact,
as we are privileged to become participants in reconciliation, we ourselves are changed. Reconciliation begins with
the healing of victims by God's grace. They, in turn, work
healing on oppressors through forgiveness, which sparks
repentance. Such reconciliation is discovered as one
becomes "tuned" through identification with the wounds
of Christ to listening and waiting, attention and compassion, and a "post-Exilic" stance whereby victims overcome
their preoccupation with oppression to become healing
agents of reconciliation. How meaningful now becomes the

dominical charge that we are not to perform the rituals of our faith while remaining unreconciled to our brother or sister (Matt. 5:23-24).

Schreiter is not overly sanguine. Sometimes reconciliation may only be an eschatological reality. Nevertheless, the task and the vision predominate like the living water, which wells up and flows out of the envisioned temple bringing refreshment and healing to all (Ezek. 47:1-12).

Few titles could be more appropriate than this one to the social reality in which many of us find ourselves. It is, therefore, with gratitude that the Boston Theological Institute (BTI) welcomes this book as the third in a series on faith and culture worldwide, growing out of our Annual Consultation on Global Mission and published jointly with Orbis Books.

RODNEY L. PETERSEN
Executive Director
Boston Theological Institute

Introduction

Stirring events in Eastern Europe, South Africa, and Latin America have pushed a topic to center stage that long had lingered in the wings: reconciliation. The struggle to overcome oppressive regimes had consumed most of the energy that individuals and communities had at their disposal until, suddenly, it appeared as though their goals had been achieved. What came after that was the difficult task of reconstruction—or better, new construction—of society. Such constructions do not happen immediately, coming full-grown from the head of Zeus, as it were. Rather, the process is painfully slow and always difficult. Part of that difficulty is the weight of the past on the present, a burden compounded by memories of violence, betrayal, and oppression. The lifting of that burden comes about through reconciliation.

Reconciliation is an intensely sought but elusive goal. Part of the difficulty is the sheer enormity of the task, so great that it seems well-nigh unachievable. For it is not only a matter of healing memories and receiving forgiveness, it is also about changing the structures in society that provoked, promoted, and sustained violence. Reconciliation is also elusive because people sometimes seek the wrong things from the wrong people at the wrong time. When should repentance be required or forgiveness sought? Can a reconciliation program be put into place?

How and when should the perpetrator of violence and the victim be brought together? Our impatience at getting beyond the sometimes unbearable burdens of the past may actually impede any possible reconciliation process as much as support it.

My own interest in the reconciliation process began in 1986 during a visit to Chile. "Reconciliation in Truth" had been written into the national pastoral plan by the Roman Catholic Bishops' Conference of that country and was the subject of much discussion. During the visit I was asked by someone who was very active in the struggle for human rights, "How do you seek reconciliation with someone who does not think he has done anything wrong?" This question struck at the very heart of the matter.

That question has never left me. With the sea changes that the world has undergone in geopolitics since 1986, the question has become more urgent. When the invitation came in 1990 from the International Missions and Ecumenism Committee of the Boston Theological Institute to give the lectures during the 1991 Orlando E. Costas Consultation on Mission on some aspect of suffering and deliverance from suffering, it was clear the time had come to try to think through the question of reconciliation more carefully.

What is presented here is an expanded version of those lectures. In such short compass, not all aspects of reconciliation can be explored. But what I have tried to do is examine some of the principal questions of concern: the relation of violence and reconciliation, a clearer understanding of the dynamics of reconciliation, the Christian understanding of reconciliation, and the church's role in the reconciliation process.

This is laid out in four chapters. The first chapter looks at the contexts in which the call for reconciliation is now being made, and the peculiar complexities of each. There is also a discussion of what reconciliation is not, since the term is coopted ideologically in some places and sometimes false expectations about reconciliation are raised. The second chapter proposes a way of looking at violence and the deliverance from suffering caused by violence. It uses a model in which narrative is the key to our sense of safety and selfhood. The third chapter proposes that the heart of the Christian understanding of reconciliation can be found in the Pauline and Deuteropauline writings of the Christian Scriptures. The insights garnered there are then brought together in five propositions that purport to catch the heart of the message of reconciliation. The fourth and final chapter looks at the church's role in the reconciliation process: both whether it has a role, and what resources it can bring to bear on the process.

The whole of the work focuses on societies experiencing a shift in their social order and the need for reconciliation as a society overcomes a violent past. Needless to say, there are many other kinds of situations that cry out for reconciliation in our societies: reconciliation between spouses, in families, among races. While a few allusions are made to these, I felt it important to keep my focus on the larger political picture. I hope that some of what is said here will be useful in those other situations as well.

As with any work such as this book, it was not accomplished alone. Thanks go first of all to Rodney Petersen, Executive Director of the Boston Theological Institute, for the invitation to give the lectures and for the conversations with him about this theme. Thanks likewise to the BTI's International Missions and Ecumenism Committee, who oversee the Consultation, and especially to Brent Armistead, its coordinator, who was my contact through the months of preparation and who organized the 1991 Consultation itself so masterfully. My interlocutors during the Consultation have helped improve the book in more ways than they know. Among them, I owe a special debt to Samuel Solivan for his insightful remarks and critique. Thomas Hemm and Jose Antonio Lagos, confreres of mine in the Society of the Precious Blood in Chile, have been conversation partners on this theme through the last several years, and what appears here bears the mark of their thoughts. And William Burrows, my tireless but immensely patient editor at Orbis Books, deserves thanks not only for seeing this book through production, but even more so for the conversations we have had on this topic.

It was a privilege for me to give these lectures for the Orlando E. Costas Consultation on Mission. I was especially happy to honor his memory in this way. He and I worked together in the American Society of Missiology, and I am sure that he would have had much to say about the topic here presented.

1

The Contexts of Reconciliation

THE END OF A WORLD ORDER

It has often been said that the twentieth century really began in August of 1914. In that fateful month Europe found itself embarking on a war that would end the political configurations of the European empires of the nineteenth century. In a similar manner, it could also be said that the twentieth century really came to an end in 1989. In that year the political arrangements that had grown out of the 1914 war and were consolidated in a second great war collapsed in a swift and dramatic fashion. Most explicitly, the end of Soviet rule in Eastern Europe and the growing disorder within the Soviet Union itself meant that the world could no longer be understood in the bipolar way that had characterized much of political consciousness for nearly fifty years. China, the great dragon of the East, shuddered and seemed also on the verge of momentous change, but those movements were to end tragically in Tiananmen Square.

The East-West political divisions, emblematic of the

struggle between communism and capitalism, captured
the most attention because of the military power lined up
along that divide. But much else had been afoot. Notably,
the move to restructuring or *perestroika* in the Soviet
Union had seemed to be the trigger that set off a chain
reaction of unforeseen restructurings elsewhere. But
apart from the the effects of *perestroika*, a number of
other developments pointed to some other fundamental
reordering of things:

The economic rise of the so-called "four dragons" in
Asia—Korea, Japan, Taiwan, and Singapore—has
reshaped the economic climate of the world and has ush-
ered in a new chapter of the global economy. The Pacific
sector is now the area of the world economy's most dramatic growth. With the addition of the stock exchanges in
Tokyo, Hong Kong, and Singapore, stock trading is now
in action at any hour of the day somewhere in the world,
a fact that has altered the pace of capital flow and the
accumulation of wealth. Although current cartography
typically represents the Atlantic Ocean at the center of
the flat maps of the world, it is likely that this old practice
could soon change as the Century of the Pacific dawns
upon us.

The resurgence of Islam in the Middle East after two
centuries of humiliation and its rapid growth in Africa
have gained it a prominence not experienced since the end
of Muslim rule in the Iberian peninsula five hundred years
ago. Many Muslims feel that they have been betrayed by
the West, and that the hoped-for advantages of embracing
modernization have not come to fruition. Consequently,
there has been a turning away from the West in many
places and a seeking of cultural revitalization in the depths
of the Muslim tradition. The migration of Muslims out of
Bangladesh, India, and Pakistan looking for better working conditions, and the flow of workers out of the Middle
East and North Africa into Europe have created new cul-

tural configurations through that whole part of the world. Muslims now are the second largest religious body in France and Italy after Roman Catholics. In the United States, Muslims constitute the seventh largest single relig- ious body (after Roman Catholics, Southern Baptists, Methodists, Lutherans, Presbyterians, and Jews.) More- over, the *daiwa* or mission of Islam makes it the fastest growing religious belief in the world today, second in size only to Christianity. The fact that so much of the world's energy reserves is in Muslim hands (in the Middle East, in Nigeria, and in Indonesia) makes the *Dar al-Islam* a new player with high stakes in the game of world order.

The resurgence of ethnic claims to sovereignty and the migration of peoples in search of better economic condi- tions are redrawing the map of cultures and peoples throughout the world. At a time when we are urged to think of the human society in global terms, local groupings are raising their voices to be heard and familiar cultural configurations are being challenged. We had become used to thinking in terms of great nation-states. But as soon as the constraints of force are relaxed only a bit, it becomes apparent that those nation-states or empires are really a mosaic of ethnic groups or nationalities. We soon remem- ber that the Soviet Union is a "union" of sixteen repub- lics, some of them in turn made up of even further subdivisions; that Yugoslavia is made up of six republics; and Czechoslovakia of three (plus a substantial Hungarian minority as well). The weakening of the military power in those places has encouraged people to rise up and assert their autonomy. The nation-state itself has been revealed to be a historical construct, not a fact of nature or of cul- ture. Indeed it was born in the late seventeenth century and may have trouble surviving deep into the twenty-first; the flow of capital and the communication of markets seem largely to have preempted many of its earlier pre- rogatives.

New world order is a much-touted term these days. But
it would be safer to say that we have seen one world order
end and have yet to see another world order take its place.
The violence that occurred in the Persian Gulf in 1990-
91 not only bespeaks the interregnum we are experiencing, it also mirrors the twentieth century. The response
to Iraq's invasion of Kuwait at first boded well of a new
way of negotiating conflict—through use of economic
rather than military force. This effectively admitted that
the language of the social order had become economic
rather than military. But new ways of thinking come
slowly to nations. Before long a reach was made for the
old rhetoric of military power, a rhetoric not changed
much since the beginning of the twentieth century. The
aerial bombings of Iraq became but a forty-five year
update of the conclusion of the Second World War in Germany and Japan. The chaos that ensued after the ceasefire
in 1991 and the continual friction over the freedom of
U.N. inspection teams showed how insufficient such military response had become to a problem of conflict, with
the flow of refugees, the uprising of the Kurds, and the
blackened skies over the Persian Gulf.

But there have been transformations in other parts of
the world as well as the twentieth century approaches its
close. During the 1980s all of the dictatorships that ruled
the overwhelming majority of South America's peoples
came to an end, with some form of democracy taking their
place. Some came to an end through an agreement to elec-
tions, others fell more violently, and still others resulted
from the military's acknowledgment that the economies
were spiralling out of control. Tragically, in most
instances, the move to democracy was not accompanied by
any real change in the economic arrangement of things;
the lot of most of the population worsened under the burden of external debt and uncontrollable inflation. Oddly
here, in Latin America, the new rhetoric of economics was

speaking more clearly than in the Northern hemisphere; the greatest constraint on returning to military rule was that the military did not wish to assume responsibility for the shambles of the national economy, a shambles to which it had largely contributed.

But beyond the violence of hunger and poverty, there was an incredible level of violence directly against human beings. Changes in government, and therefore the setting up of the possibility for a new social order, were preceded by protracted civil wars in Central America, by the violence of the ideology of the national security state in Brazil and Paraguay, and the violence of the waves and counter-waves of insurgents and military with civilians caught in between in Peru. A new term came into the language of societal conflict: *to disappear,* a euphemism for the abduction of civilians whose fates were thus virtually sealed.

Africa, too, knew inconceivable violence through the closing decades of the twentieth century. Much of its political map had begun to take shape at the 1885 conference in Berlin, with no Africans present. Political boundaries cut through ethnic territories, dividing some groups among two and three countries and throwing them together with long-standing enemies as new civic bedfellows. The results have been tragic for Africa, with ethnic rivalries regularly boiling over into civil wars that waste the precious human resources of those countries. There have been seventy coups against African governments in the first thirty years of independence.

The civil wars represent one of the three tragic ways that Africa has been depleted of its human resources and thus had its development hindered. The first was the European and American slave trade from the sixteenth through the nineteenth centuries. The second is this perduring state of interethnic warfare. And the third is the spread of the AIDS epidemic across central Africa.

In southern Africa another word was added to the

vocabulary of societal conflict: *apartheid*. While there is hope that the legislation that supported the ideology of racial separation is coming to end, the conditions that make it possible and that sustain it in fact if not in law remain firmly in place.

The seventy-five years from 1914 to 1989 that make up the twentieth century have been uncommonly violent, costing the planet millions of lives in war and the consequences of war. Indeed, the times have been so violent that to speak of "world order" has an oddly oxymoronic ring to it.

That violence has been of three types: war between nation-states or among groups of nation-states; war among cultural groups or between ideologies within states; and that which allows the ideologies of colonialism and racism to sustain structures that do violence to peoples in subtle and not so subtle ways. The first type has given us the bloody wars that have often engaged large parts of the planet. The second type has given us both civil wars, which often have been no less bloody than their larger counterparts, and patterns of domination that wreak their own kind of violence upon peoples through the structures and systems of so-called security. And the third type carries on war by other means, masking itself as peace. All have conspired to make this century surely one of the most violent that humankind has seen.

We find ourselves now, it would seem, between the times. We do not know how long this liminal situation will last, nor exactly what will take its place. The conflict in the Persian Gulf has not inspired confidence in our ability to construct a new and better world order. And a new order has not arisen phoenix-like from the ashes of Eastern European societies. We are always, it seems, impatient with ambiguity. Dwelling precisely in that ambiguity may be necessary to keep us from simply repeating the past.

Being between the times can jar our awareness enough

to reflect on who we have become and where we might go. That is in itself a formidable task. This is especially so in view of the blood-soaked century closing out behind us. The purpose of the reflections offered here is to explore one facet of that task that emerges for us in our liminal *transitional* situation — to examine how people move from a situation of violence and suffering into something new and different. Our first impulse may be to envision the move from violence and suffering as a step back to the way things might have been prior to the cataclysmic events that have wracked our societies and our lives. And some peoples have tried to do that. But a little experience and a little reflection teach us rather quickly that it is not possible. It is not only that the flow of time makes retrieving the past ultimately impossible; it is also that the experience of vio- *LOTR* lence and suffering has changed us irrevocably. We are not the same people we were, and so any return is not a return; it is coming into a new place. Those who have found themselves in the midst of war and violence, who have experienced the terrors of violence, cannot return to a prior, tranquil state. The violence of those times is burned into memory — repressed perhaps, but surely able to come to the surface once again to haunt and horrify the present.

Violence has been so much part of the recent world order, and is still so much with us, that to think about a new and better world order requires that we dwell on that peculiar feature of our times. A move to a new world order cannot be made by simply ignoring or repressing the memory of that violent past; indeed, not to remember what has happened will likely mean that we will end up inventing new ways of continuing that cycle of violence. Rather, the challenge is how to come to terms with violence and suffering, particularly the violence and suffering in regimes that have or are now collapsing with the end of the twentieth-century world order, and then develop a different kind of world, a world that truly moves beyond violence into genuine peace. How shall a redemption from suffering and violence take place that will effect a genuine reconciliation — in other words, offer the conditions under which a more just and more peaceful society might come about?

Reconciliation, then, will be the focus of our reflections here. From what has already been said, it should be clear that considerable thought will have to be given to the antecedents of reconciliation before the moment of reconciliation can be achieved. Indeed it is those antecedents of reconciliation, namely, the redemption from violence and suffering, that form the preoccupation of this book. This is so because all too often there are quick and superficial calls for reconciliation, often by those who stand outside the cycle of violence and suffering. These come from people who are deeply uncomfortable with conflict, for a variety of reasons to be detailed below. Sometimes, too, the call for reconciliation comes from those who have been the oppressors or the perpetrators of violence, in the hopes that they will be spared punishment. Hence reconciliation in all its difficulty will be the object of our investigation.

The concern here is not just reconciliation in its general form. It has to do with what the Christian message brings to the process of reconciliation and what role the churches might play in that process. The term *reconciliation* may not figure prominently as a theme in the scriptures, but as a theme it runs like a red thread through all the sacred texts. For is not the story of salvation the story of God's reconciling the world to God's self?

The churches have historically played roles in reconciliation processes — both because of their power in civil society and, more important, because of the messages they bear from Christ to be agents of reconciliation. To explore a bit further this latter point about the role of the churches in the process of reconciliation, let me give a few examples of situations where people are pondering these things today.

The collapse of Communist domination in countries in Eastern Europe raises a host of questions about a new order. In most of those countries the church cannot escape the question of reconciliation because the fault-line of violence runs right through the church itself. In Czechoslovakia and Hungary, for example, what will be done with those Roman Catholic priests who were part of the so-called peace groups, officially sanctioned by a Communist regime that was at the same time imprisoning other Roman Catholics? How shall they relate to those who suffered imprisonment and other violence for their commitments to the Roman Catholic Church? Can they be reconciled to each other?

Or how shall Catholics and Orthodox be reconciled in the Ukraine? Here the political regime is still in place, though it has relaxed its opposition to religious faith. The Ukrainian Catholic Church was suppressed, its leadership imprisoned or executed, and its property confiscated under Stalin. Its membership was forcibly merged into the Ukrainian Orthodox Church. While the Orthodox church also suffered cruelly under the regime, it was not faced with a program of extinction. Now, in a climate less hostile to religion in general, Ukrainian Catholics are reemerging from a kind of underground. How shall those who resisted assimilation into the Orthodox church relate to those who did not and now wish to return to the Catholic church? Even more difficult, how shall Catholics and Orthodox live together in the future? Is reconciliation possible?

A somewhat similar situation is present in the People's Republic of China, where the government has given greater freedom to certain forms of religious expression. For Protestant Christians, there are divisions between Christians who are part of the postdenominational China Christian Council and some of those in the house churches, which see those who collaborate with the government as traitors to Christian faith. The divisions among Catholics have been even sharper, between those who worship in churches that have some measure of government recognition (because of present or past connections with the Catholic Patriotic Association) and those who are in the so-called underground church. The latter still risk arrest and imprisonment, as do some of those in Protestant house churches. Is reconciliation possible?

Violence such as that experienced in Eastern Europe is not the only variety to be found. In South Africa, where the violent structures of apartheid are slowly being dismantled, questions arise about how reconciliation between races might come about when those structures are gone: What of the victims of torture and exile, and the masses of people forcibly relocated into the "homelands"? And what should happen to those black persons who collaborated with the racist regime? Where should the church try to be in all of this?

Chile represents another kind of situation, where a country that had the longest history of democratic rule in South America is now just emerging from a violent, seventeen-year dictatorship. Here the lines of violence did not run along racial lines, nor did the ideological divide run through the church. Indeed, the Roman Catholic Church was the one force powerful enough to confront the Pinochet regime during its bloody seventeen-year rule. But now, as the mass graves of those executed under the regime are being opened, as the exiles and refugees return, and the Aylwin government has released its report on crimes committed in the Pinochet years, how shall the nation be healed?

And then there are the situations in postcolonial Africa, where conflicts among peoples organized artificially into nation-states erupt in bloody civil wars that do not get resolved as much as they exhaust themselves in destruction. The conflicts in Liberia and Uganda are only the most recent. One remembers those in Zaire in the 1960s, and in Nigeria and Burundi into the 1970s, only to name some of the most violent. Can reconciliation happen when structures that encourage violence have not been changed?

The list could, of course, be lengthened even further. One thinks of the struggle in the Philippines or the killing fields of Cambodia. But these examples do raise in different ways the questions before us: Is reconciliation possible? And if so, how? In each of these cases cited, the Christian church finds itself already implicated. In the case of Czechoslovakia and Hungary, the Roman Catholic Church must deal with those who collaborated with a regime that has now been replaced with one more friendly to religious faith. What should be done with those who collaborated with the hostile regime, perhaps with good intentions of finding as much room as possible for faith in such an environment? In some instances the collaboration is seen as intolerable. Indeed, because of such collaboration, the patriarch of the Roumanian Orthodox Church felt constrained to resign.

This is different but still similar to the situation in the Ukraine and China, where the hostile governments are still in place but have taken a more relaxed view of religious faith and are allowing public religious activity. There too the questions have to do with believers and leaders who have chosen different strategies to make religious activity possible: some by direct and complete resistance to the regime; others by collaborating in order to keep some measure of public activity alive.

South Africa presents another kind of situation, where the different Christian churches have found themselves on both sides of the apartheid question, but where many of the churches have taken active roles in the struggle against apartheid. Here certain laws have been taken away, but it is still uncertain about what will take their place. Moreover, racism will continue to function despite new legislation. And how shall torturers and the tortured come to live together? Can peace among races ever be established? On what conditions? What does Christian faith contribute to building a new order?

Chile offers a situation where the church took the front line of resistance to a regime and now, in a return to democracy, must help bring about reconciliation among people trying to live together again. Here it is a case of trying to live together under the old rules (that is, democracy) rather than something new. Poland represents a somewhat different though similar case.

Each of these examples brings forth a different complexity, even in the very broad outlines in which they have been sketched here. Below the surfaces of those outlines even greater complexities lurk. For example, in the situation among Catholics in China, the dividing line of loyalty to the pope that established the split in 1958 is in many cases now very hard to discern. Many if not most so-called Patriotic Catholics consider themselves loyal to the Holy See. Changes mandated by the Second Vatican Council and the Holy See are being implemented even in Patriotic institutions.

Moreover, it is not only a matter of discerning where the lines of division run in each of these situations, or of how improved the larger situation is in which reconciliation must take place. How to bring the sides together is complicated by other factors. Principally, this problem is most evident in the realization that some of the actors in these tragic dramas do not feel that they have done anything wrong, and that therefore reconciliation is not even an issue. Those church people who collaborated with an oppressive regime might see themselves as having kept the churches alive. Those who worked for regimes—for example, in Chile—may see themselves as having saved the nation from communism. Those on the other side of the question and those outside the situation may judge such

persons otherwise, but the fact remains that some do not
feel guilt for what they did.

It is within these shifting and confusing parameters
that I would like to explore the theme of reconciliation,
recognizing full-well the complexities of the topic and the
partial character of the responses offered here to those
complexities. But living when we do — between the times — *what times?*
we cannot permit ourselves to be paralyzed either by the
complexity or the awesome size of the task. How does one
respond to the thousands of deaths, to the mass graves,
to the victims of torture whose lives can never be the
same, and to the families that have suffered damage that
cannot be completely repaired? We are numbed nearly into
silence before the enormity of violence that has been perpetrated upon peoples just within our lifetimes.

But as Christians we cannot just stand by helplessly.
Does not our Christian faith speak of redemption, of liberation, even of forgiveness of enemies? What does the
message of Jesus contribute to the building of a new order
in those situations that have been dominated by so much
violence? What do Christians mean by reconciliation?

The scope of this book does not allow for a complete
treatment of this complex theme. Rather, it will focus on
two areas within that process. It will attend first of all to
the role of violence and suffering, and the redemption
from both violence and suffering, that lie at the heart of
the reconciliation process. Reconciliation cannot be understood without coming to terms with violence and suffering. Second, this book will explore just what we Christians
mean by reconciliation and what will be entailed for the
Christian church to be an agent of reconciliation. For the
heart of the Christian message — our deliverance from sin
and the forces of evil, and God's offer of new life — is certainly at the center in this concern for understanding better the meaning of reconciliation. Indeed as we may recall,
it was the concept *reconciliation* that Karl Barth used to

draw together his theology of God's activity in Christ in the fourth part of the *Church Dogmatics*.

In the rest of this first chapter I wish to explore one theme: what reconciliation is not. Part of dealing with the complexity of what reconciliation means is clearing the ground, as it were, of mistaken notions.

WHAT RECONCILIATION IS NOT

There is some advantage at beginning the study of a concept by saying what it is not, lest the wrong connotations cling to it. That is certainly the case with reconciliation, since the word is used in many different ways. We can speak of reconciling bank statements, reconciliation in a labor union dispute, reconciling contradictory facts, reconciliation in a divorce suit, or even reconciliation of sinners. We can more or less assume that these are not the ways reconciliation is being used here, since our concern is reconciliation of a social order, especially after a period of violence. But as we have seen, even within the contexts of creating a new social order, reconciliation can be misused to avoid the fact of conflict or to shield those who were perpetrators of violence.

And it is precisely those misunderstandings of reconciliation that need to be named and addressed here. There are at least three understandings of reconciliation that come close to the genuine meaning of reconciliation but distort and even falsify its true sense. These three are: reconciliation as a hasty peace, reconciliation instead of liberation, and reconciliation as a managed process. Let us look at each of these three in turn.

Reconciliation as a Hasty Peace

The first form of false reconciliation tries to deal with a history of violence by suppressing its memory. By not adverting to the fact that violence has taken place, this approach is supposed to put the violent history behind us and allow us to begin afresh. Not surprisingly, this kind of reconciliation is often called for by the very perpetrators of violence who, either having seen what they have done or having realized the potential consequences of their actions, want to get on to a new and different situation. They want the victims of violence to let bygones be bygones and exercise a Christian forgiveness. While reconciliation as a hasty peace bears a superficial resemblance to Christian reconciliation, it is actually quite far from it.

James H. Cone gave an excellent analysis of this kind of reconciliation at the end of his *Black Theology and Black Power*. Cone responded to those who would replace Black Power with a theology of reconciliation with, "Yeah, what about it, man?" Such calls for reconciliation not only trivialize and ignore the sufferings that African Americans have undergone, but also ignore the source of the sufferings — namely, those who oppress and do violence to African Americans, and now call for love and integration, are members of one and the same group: white people.[1]

In trivializing and ignoring a history of suffering, such false attempts at reconciliation actually underscore how far the situation still is from a genuine reconciliation. By calling on those who have suffered to forget or overlook their suffering, the would-be reconcilers are in fact continuing the oppressive situation by saying, in effect, that the experiences of those who suffered are not important — and therefore they themselves are unimportant to the process. To trivialize and ignore memory is to trivialize and ignore human identity, and to trivialize and ignore human identity is to trivialize and ignore human dignity. That is why reconciliation as a hasty peace is actually the opposite of reconciliation. By forgetting the suffering, the victim is forgotten and the causes of suffering are never uncovered and confronted.

Moreover, reconciliation as a hasty peace tries to escape an examination of the causes of suffering. If the causes of suffering are not addressed, suffering is likely to continue; the wheel of violence keeps turning, and more and more people get crushed. Reconciliation, as we shall see, is a process that cannot be foreshortened; it keeps its own timetables.

A quick way to identify this kind of false reconciliation is to look at who is calling for reconciliation and what they want forgotten. Sometimes those calling for such a reconciliation are well-meaning but naive outsiders, not the direct perpetrators of violence. Such well-meaning people may also contribute to the violence by their actions, since they are allying themselves with the perpetrators of violence in the way that they are addressing themselves to the victims of violence. Unfortunately church leaders sometimes cast themselves in this role, thinking they are doing the Christian thing. They stress correctly the theme of Christian forgiveness, but are ignorant in this situation of what forgiveness will entail.

What can be learned about true reconciliation from this false kind of reconciliation? Certainly we see that reconciliation is not a hasty process, and that it is one that requires respecting—and often restoring—the human dignity of the victim of violence. Moreover, it opens the question of where a call to genuine reconciliation must originate. While many may hope for reconciliation, there are really only certain people who have the moral authority to issue the call for reconciliation. These few may be moral authorities that both sides respect (that is the assumption that underlies the attempts of church leaders to make this call). But, somewhat paradoxically, it is more likely to come from those who have suffered most in the situation. The reason for this, quite simply, is that we cannot forgive ourselves for the wrongdoing of our past. Those whom we have injured must do that. Not to realize this is to confuse reconciliation with repentance. Repentance can originate from the side of those who have perpetrated violence, but reconciliation and forgiveness must come from the side of those who have suffered violence.

Reconciliation as a hasty peace, while often motivated by an urge to get beyond violence, is not true reconciliation. It covers up the enormity of what has been done and tries to foreshorten the process. It is often driven by the fear that remembering the violence of the past will lead to a new outbreak of hostility. But suppressing the memory does not take the violence away; it only postpones its expurgation. Such an attempt grows out of a fundamental misunderstanding of the process of reconciliation, not realizing that there is more to reconciliation than a cessation of violence. Reconciliation involves a fundamental repair to human lives, especially to the lives of those who have suffered. That repair takes time—time that can make the participants feel insecure, but necessary time nonetheless for beginning a new life.

Reconciliation Instead of Liberation

In 1985 the president of CELAM, the organization of Roman Catholic Bishops' Conferences in Latin America, made the suggestion that reconciliation, not liberation, was the proper theme for Latin American theology and praxis. The suggestion, whatever its import, was followed quickly by conferences organized by conservative church leaders exploring reconciliation as a theme at the heart of genuine Christian praxis.

Similar to the understanding of reconciliation as a hasty peace, there is some truth to seeing reconciliation as the heart of the Christian message. The hymns in Colossians and Ephesians certainly portray reconciliation as the center of God's plan for creation. In this light reconciliation could be considered superior to liberation in that libera-

tion says more about what we are rescued from than about
what we are destined to. Reconciliation has connotations
of that blessed state to which we all are called. It also
seems to enshrine the Christian belief in love of enemies
that lies close to the heart of the Christian message.

The *Kairos Document*, published in 1985 by concerned
South African theologians, points to the fallacy that is
masked behind the assertion that Christians should talk
of reconciliation instead of liberation. Latin American theologians such as José Comblin have analyzed the misunderstanding of Christian reconciliation here as well.[2] Put
simply, liberation is not an alternative to reconciliation; it
is the prerequisite for it. Thus, we do not call for reconciliation instead of liberation; we call for liberation in
order to bring about reconciliation. Not liberation *or* reconciliation. Rather, no reconciliation without liberation.
Reconciliation can only come about if the nature of the
violence perpetrated is acknowledged, and its conditions
for continuing or reappearing are removed. Liberation is
not just liberation from the violent situation, but also liberation from the structures and processes that permit and
promote violence. To choose reconciliation as an alternative to liberation does not acknowledge the deeply conflictive realities that create the chasms that reconciliation
hopes to bridge. It also presumes that violence is quickly
and easily overcome.

This is particularly the case in situations where the violence is covert—or at least not overt to part of the population. Such is the case with the violence of racism. In the
United States, for example, white people sometimes cannot understand the anger of black people since the white
people are not aware of the dynamics of racism in which
they themselves participate. Hence, as illustrated above in
the reference to the early work of James Cone, they called
for integration instead of Black Power. What they failed
to realize is that integration was on the whites' terms and

did not take into account the need to change some fundamental structures in society. Hispanic peoples in the United States often suffer deeply from racism as well, sometimes of an even more deleterious nature since Anglos do not even recognize their reactions are motivated by racism.

What can be learned about the nature of true reconciliation from this false juxtaposition of liberation versus reconciliation? First of all, conflict is not peripheral to the reconciliation process but is met at its very heart. If the sources of conflict are not named, examined, and taken away, reconciliation will not come about. What we will have is a truce, not a peace. This is the fact that those who have perpetrated violence or have been witting or unwitting accessories to the violence find difficult to accept. Churches fall easy prey to this, since they are rarely the direct violators. It is often their silence, not their words, that makes them participants in the violation of those who suffer. The voices of those who suffer then become a very unwelcome sound to their ears because they are made uncomfortable.

Second, juxtaposing liberation to reconciliation bespeaks a worldview or understanding of reality that, by itself, can block the reconciliation process. It assumes a consensus rather than conflictive view of the world. Churches often want to function only in a consensus model of reality that emphasizes harmony and harmonization of conflicting interests. This is understandable inasmuch as the love of God and neighbor lies at the heart of the gospel. The idyllic picture in Acts 4 of the church living in utter harmony informs much of the Christian self-image. Indeed, one of the major objections of the Vatican against Latin American liberation theology is its promotion of a view of the world and humanity that does not grow out of this worldview.

While all of us would like to live in such a peaceful and

harmonious world, we do not. Most of us live out our lives experiencing reality as conflict, whether the direct conflict of overt domination or the more covert realities of racism or sexism. While we can maintain that a genuinely Christian anthropology or view of humanity should not or cannot be based on a conflictive view of reality, such language has little hope for acceptance if somehow conflict, and the causes of conflict, are not met and addressed.[3] Genuine reconciliation must meet conflict and face its causes squarely.

Is a conflictive view of humanity compatible with Christianity? Our first reaction would probably be to say no. To support a conflictive view of humanity is to admit that conflict is of the essence of our being, and so reconciliation is neither necessary nor possible. It would also seem to give a warrant to those who wish to perpetrate violence by legitimating belief in the innate inferiority of some people to others. Leninism and some forms of Maoism are built on such beliefs. But to consign conflictive views of reality to these extreme forms is to fail to differentiate between different views of conflict, for we can have a conflictive view of reality that does not require conflict as the ultimate meaning and purpose of life. After all, the Christian story of salvation would be unintelligible without such a view. Christians say that God brought about reconciliation through the death of Christ. That reconciliation was needed, and that it took such an extreme measure to be achieved as the violent death of Christ hardly bespeaks a consensus view of reality: "And through him [Jesus] God was pleased to reconcile to himself all things, whether on earth or in heaven, by making peace through the blood of his cross" (Col. 1:20). We can hold to a conflictive view of reality without making conflict the ultimate shape of that reality. This is essentially what Christianity does. It acknowledges the enmity between God and the world, and that this enmity will be overcome completely somehow in the future, eschatologically. Perhaps it would be better to say that not only *may* a Christian hold to a conflictive view of reality, but a Christian *must* hold to such a view in order to acknowledge sin and evil in the world and to participate in the process of overcoming it.

Seen this way, it becomes apparent why reconciliation cannot be offered as an alternative to liberation. Liberation is the necessary precondition for reconciliation. Consequently, calls for reconciliation can provide a goal for liberation, but they cannot replace it.

Reconciliation as a Managed Process

Genuine reconciliation is also confused at times with conflict mediation, a process whose goal is to lessen conflict or to get the parties to accept and live with the conflictual situation. Reconciliation of this type is seen as being brought about by a disciplined process in which a skilled mediator helps the conflicting parties recognize the issues at conflict as representing different interests and values that have to be negotiated. Reconciliation then becomes a process of bargaining in which both sides are expected to accede some of their interests in order to reach an end to conflict. The process acknowledges that both sides have legitimate interests, but that both sets of interests cannot be met in a finite world. Consequently, a balancing process must be undertaken that will require both sides to give something up, but not give up so much that the conflict flares up again. This model is familiar in claim disputes between parties, contract negotiation between labor and management, and in coalition building in community organization settings.

Again, reconciliation as a managed process bears some resemblance to Christian reconciliation. In reconciliation as a managed process, there is an acknowledgment that people can come into conflict trying to maintain legitimate interests and values, but that these interests and values can put them hopelessly at odds with each another. Likewise, the managed process assumes that a minimum sense of human dignity for all parties in the conflict must be acknowledged, so that claims by the parties may be taken seriously. This approach also assumes that reconciliation is not a quick process, and that certain conditions must be met if the conflict is not to occur again.

But reconciliation as a managed process falls short of the Christian understanding of reconciliation in significant ways. First of all—as we shall see in more detail in Chapter 3—we do not bring about reconciliation, especially in the profound and complex situations described above; it is God who reconciles. This is not said to create an attitude of acquiescence in the face of violence or fatalism in the midst of political oppression. It is, rather, to acknowledge the enormity of the task of reconciliation in situations where the social order has shifted radically and dramatically.

Second, this approach to reconciliation reduces reconciliation to a technical rationality; it becomes a skill that can be taught to deal with a problem that can be managed. North Americans and others who live in technology-rich societies may be prone to accept this understanding of reconciliation, but it departs significantly from a biblical understanding in which reconciliation is not a skill to be mastered, but rather, something discovered—the power of God's grace welling up in one's life. This is a somewhat subtle point that will be dealt with in more detail in the third chapter. Reconciliation becomes more of an attitude than an acquired skill; it becomes a stance assumed before a broken world rather than a tool to repair that world. Or put in more theological terms, reconciliation is more spirituality than strategy.

Third, to see reconciliation as a form of technical rationality, a skill or know-how, is to reduce reconciliation to the form it takes in one kind of culture. To reduce a complex process such as reconciliation to technical rationality is a sign of respect for the purpose of that process in a technology-rich culture, such as the United States. By making reconciliation a skill it is accorded the highest (read: most scientific) form of rationality. But to reduce reconciliation to the technical-rational is to devalue it in other cultures.

We have devoted here considerable attention to what the Christian meaning of reconciliation is not. By so doing, it is my hope that the ground is cleared somewhat for exploring its full meaning. That reconciliation is accorded such a central place in the Christian message — as a way of describing God's plan for creation and Christ's central work within that plan — should alert us to how profound its meaning is likely to be. By saying what it is not, we can at least disabuse ourselves of incomplete and inauthentic meanings, and so prepare ourselves to receive its genuine meaning.

2

Violence and Suffering: Narratives of the Lie

THE QUEST FOR SAFETY AND SELFHOOD

In the previous chapter we looked at some of the definitional ramifications of reconciliation, especially at what reconciliation is not. We turn now to one dimension of reconciliation that is the focus of this book, namely, the deliverance from violence and suffering caused by violence into a process of reconciliation. As is already becoming apparent, there are many dimensions to the reconciliation process: its contexts, the roles of the various actors in the process, attitudes and values to be kept in mind. We saw that the contexts for the reconciliation process can be quite varied due to the course of events and the nature of the violence perpetrated. There are a variety of actors, too: those oppressed, those involved directly in oppressing, those who are witting and unwitting accessories to the oppressors. Likewise, in looking at what reconciliation is not, we uncovered values and attitudes that both should and should not come into play.

One element is especially difficult to deal with in the reconciliation process: the violence perpetrated upon individuals, families, and whole societies that causes such great suffering. It is perhaps the most painful and terrifying aspect of the reconciliation process with which we must deal.

Violence takes on many forms. The most obvious is direct physical violence, which involves assault on an individual or a group. But there is indirect physical violence too, for example, withholding resources to the point of starvation. The oppression of peoples economically is an example of this. Then there are psychic sorts of violence that wreak havoc on a person's self-concept or self-esteem. Racism is a particularly virulent form of this violence, wherein a group is told over and over again this it is inferior to some other group. How are we to confront these kinds of violence and the suffering they cause? How are we delivered from them? In this chapter I would like to dwell particularly on how we come to terms with violence as a step in the reconciliation process.

Violence itself is a deeply destructive event in both individuals and communities. Its corrosive effects upon the fragile webs of meaning we weave about ourselves can cause us to think of it as irrational and, therefore, unsuitable for any response except either counterviolence or flight. But violence is not irrational. It has its own rationality, one that is supremely rational but counterrational to those ordinary rationalities that create and sustain meaning in our lives. While the violence of nature may have little rationality, the violence of oppressive governments has a rationality aimed precisely at the destruction of existent and opposing rationalities. The contest, however, is not carried out at the level of concepts. Rather, the struggle touches those very things that make us human and keep us from sliding into oblivion. That is why violence is so terrifying and why its effects are so difficult to overcome.

To get at the question of violence, then, we must find a way of conceiving of violence, of getting at its peculiar rationality. Following the work of anthropologist René Girard (but developing it in a slightly different way), I would like to suggest a way of conceiving violence and the suffering that comes from it. From that a way can be constructed to reach out for a redeeming liberation that rescues us from the clutches of that violence.

Girard has proposed that a violent act lies at the formation of every culture or society. That violence explains why every society is inherently unstable and why societies resort to violence as a way of dealing with conflict. This is an unprovable hypothesis, but it does provide an account of why violence recurs in societies. While I do not follow out his theory completely, he does provide important insights into the nature of violence that are of use here.[4]

We must begin by realizing what fragile constructions we humans and our societies are. We are largely bereft of instinct and so feel deeply insecure in an uncertain and often dangerous world. Not only do we feel uncertain and insecure, we are not told who we are. We need to find our selves and to check them constantly against surrounding reality. To remedy this sense of vulnerability and to avoid perishing in fear, we need to construct and reconstruct constantly for ourselves a sense of safety and a sense of selfhood.

It is our symbol-making activities that give us the capacity to construct those senses of safety and selfhood. They make up for what we lack in instinct. They do this by assigning meaning to both the physical features and the temporal events in our lives. Thus, what we eat and do not eat, what kinds of shelters we build for ourselves, what kinds of clothing we design for our bodies and how and when we wear them — all of these things are fraught with meaning. These meanings give our lives definition, a sense of sameness that reassures us of who we are and how we fit into things. That reassurance gives us a certain sense of safety that permits us to shift our attention elsewhere. That sense of sameness, which grows out of those clutches of meaning, gives rise to our definition of ourselves as selves. Our selfhood in turn guides us through the flow of time. It becomes a point of reference, providing us a sense of location and orientation in the flow of time. Because the self is so constructed, it can change through encounter with new events, even though it remains substantially the same. Because it is constructed, it is also very fragile.

The record of the encounters of the self with events is preserved for us largely in narratives — the stories that we tell about ourselves, both to ourselves and to others. These stories become foundational not only for describing ourselves to others, but for our very understanding of ourselves. They constitute our truths. They tell us what we need to know about ourselves, how we remember what has happened to us, how we may have changed, and how we have stayed the same — in other words, how we manage to be who we are.

To be sure, no individual and no culture ever really remain the same. We are drawn along constantly in the flux of change, which is why the story is never quite told the same way and indeed changes over time. It is added to, it is modified, it receives different emphases. Thus how we tell the story changes as our accumulated experience changes. It is not surprising that in the foundational story for Christians we have four gospel narratives instead of just one; we need to be able to grow and adjust to our changing world, and so our founding narrative needs to have some flexibility.

Violence is an attack on our sense of safety and selfhood. The pain that ensues goes beyond the physical pain of the assault. By being attacked we are reminded of how vulnerable we are. Continuing attacks may cause us to doubt and even abandon the narratives that encode our senses of safety and selfhood, since they do not seem to offer the assurance we seek in the midst of these onslaughts.

Torture and other forms of physical assault are systematic attempts to undermine a personal sense of safety by violating our most symbol-laden possession, our body. Often victims of torture are stripped in the torture process, a gesture that emphasizes the vulnerability we all experience just below the surface of our lives. The physical assault robs us of our selfhood; we are treated as a lump of organic material that can be manipulated at will. In another way, imprisonment and exile deliberately cut the social bonds that tie us to the story we share with others. They say, in effect, that we have been cut out of the narrative, we are no longer part of it. Acts of terrorism prey upon our story in yet another way. By undermining our sense of safety, they are calculated to make us doubt the cohesion of our narratives. They remind us of how fragile our stories are and how they can be interrupted and exploded at any time.

Pain ensues from acts of violence, but the pain that is registered psychically as our symbols are ripped apart is suffering. Pain and suffering, then, are not the same thing.

Suffering is the human struggle with and against pain. It is the experience of the breakdown of our systems of meaning and our stories about ourselves, and the struggle to restore those senses of safety and selfhood. Suffering in itself is neither noble nor redeeming. It is essentially an erosion of meaning. It is an interruption and destruction of those fundamental senses of safety and selfhood without which we cannot survive as individuals and as societies. Suffering only becomes redemptive or ennobling when we struggle against these corroding powers and rebuild our selves in spite of the pain we are experiencing. And, as we shall see, that is most likely to happen when we are able to link our narrative to other, larger narratives. Such a linkage does not happen automatically. If an individual or a society's sense of safety and selfhood is already weak, if the narratives of their identity are halting and inconclusive, the pain they suffer may become such that they literally do not survive.

VIOLENCE AS A NARRATIVE OF THE LIE

Violence tries to destroy the narratives that sustain people's identities and substitute narratives of its own. These might be called narratives of the lie, precisely because they are intended to negate the truth of a people's own narratives. The negation is evident often in the choice of Orwellian language. In Eastern Europe, for example, violence against organized religion was sustained by "peace" priests in Czechoslovakia. Violence is perpetrated against individuals to maintain state "security." Newspapers providing the ideological line of the oppressor might be called "The Truth" (*Pravda*). Black people in South Africa are uprooted from their homes to be resettled in "homelands." The negation is intended not only to destroy the narrative of the victim, but to pave the way for the oppressor's narrative. What is at issue here is the fact that we humans cannot survive without a narrative of identity. Without some narrative, we slide into a chaos that is death for animals without instincts. That is why narratives — any narratives — are better than no narratives at all. The purpose of torture, imprisonment, and coercion is not to end narratives — that is done most efficiently by simple execution — but to provide another narrative so that people will learn to live with and acquiesce to the will of the oppressor.

Not to accept the narrative of the lie means resisting

the breakdown of our own narrative. If people are imprisoned, they are physically cut off from their larger social narrative. The confinement to a restricted physical space underlines their lack of freedom to construct a sense of selfhood by their own will. To resist the acceptance of the oppressor's narratives and to protest the attempts at the destruction of their own, prisoners, especially in solitary confinement, reinforce their narratives with other narratives, any constructed string of meanings—multiplication tables, verb conjugations, lists, anything connected. To give up the connecting power of narrative in a situation of forced isolation is to slip into non-meaning and non-identity, psychosis.

Memory is another means of keeping connected to our own narrative. Remembering important events, reconstructing conversations, and recalling feelings become handholds in a precarious situation. Some ways are ingenious. A man I met several years ago had spent six months in solitary confinement in one of Chilean dictator Augusto Pinochet's jails. One of the ways that he kept sane was the assurance he had that his wife would be standing outside the prison wall every day at half past three in the afternoon. Even though he could not see her, knowing that she was there kept him connected into the larger narrative of his life.

The alternate narrative, the narrative of the lie, is the key to maintaining violent control. The assumption is that the lie will come to be accepted as the truth if the original narrative can be suppressed or at least coopted. Any attempt on the part of a population to return to its older, favored narratives is met with violence or the threat of violence. Random violence also may be used to punctuate the fragility of a population's safety. Thus, oppressive governments will routinely do random arrests or conduct nighttime raids on poor neighborhoods as a way of undermining safety and belief in any narrative except that of the government. Terrorist groups such as the *sendero luminoso* in Peru stage random executions among villagers to undermine their sense of security.

It is no wonder that in Jewish and Christian traditions the power of evil, the devil, is associated with the lie. The root meaning of the Hebrew word *Satan* is "the one who accuses falsely," and of the Greek *diabolos* is "the confuser."

THE QUEST OF A REDEEMING NARRATIVE

How do we actually overcome the suffering caused by such violence and move to reconciliation and forgiveness? First, let us concentrate only on the overcoming of suffering caused by violence. That involves overcoming the narrative of the lie, a narrative that insinuates its way into our individual and collective psyches by coiling itself around our most basic senses of security and self. It is only when we discover and embrace a redeeming narrative that we can be liberated from the lie's seductive and cunning power. Discovery and acceptance of a redeeming narrative is not an easy task, but it is a necessary one if we are to be delivered from the effects of violence upon our individual and collective psyches. If we are to deal with the suffering from violence, and not let it corrode our sense of safety and self but rather be turned into a force that gives us strength to withstand it, a different set of narratives must be found. And only then, when some sense of spiritual survival has been established, are we able to think of forgiveness, are we able to think of reconciliation.

We overcome suffering from violence by working our way through it. It is a process, therefore, but not necessarily an orderly one. We begin by acknowledging the violence that is being done to us, and we cry out in protest and lament against it. Silence is the friend of oppression and crying out names the perpetrator of the violence against us. Crying out gives voice to our pain and calls others to our side, to help us be restored to the larger social network. Crying out is an address, an appeal to God that what we face reaches beyond our ability to cope. It is in this awareness of our helplessness (particularly if the violence has cut very deeply into our sense of safety and selfhood) that we become able to accept other narratives to counteract the narrative of the lie. Our own narratives lie in disarray and, even if reconstructed, cannot be the same again. We need to find other narratives that can pick up the fragments of our own and piece them back together.

We need, then, to find an *orthopathema*, a right way to suffer, when our orthodoxies have been shattered and our orthopraxies have come to naught.[5] Our orthodoxies, our right ways of believing, have been replaced in violence with a heterodoxy, another way of believing—the narrative of the lie. Our orthopraxies have been countered by another way of acting. At the heart of the *orthopathema* is an act of fundamental trust, a faith, in the new narrative. That fundamental trust must be at the same level and at the same intensity that allowed us to believe in those symbols and narratives that first shaped our identity. For that act of trusting reveals our humanity at its most real and its most vulnerable. It is indeed both that which makes us human and that which has been so profoundly betrayed by acts of violence. Our societies are built upon trust; violence attempts to negate that.

A right way of suffering, then, involves regaining our humanity. Violence is aimed precisely at stripping us of our humanity, of that which distinguishes us from the other animals—that network of meaning that is our sense of safety and self. By denying the meanings we construct we are left with little but our instincts to guard us, and they are very weak. We are offered the narrative of the lie to replace our own narratives, a twisted narrative that will keep us in a subdued, subhuman state if we accept it. It checks our ability to trust and makes us suspicious of everyone. The use of terrorist police squads and informers in totalitarian states is aimed especially at undermining any ability to trust.

The nucleus of our humanity is restored to us in reestablishing the ability to trust. This can be a long and delicate process. Both preceding that ability to trust and accompanying its unfolding is a reconstruction of memory. Memory is the principal repository of our identity. We turn to memory to know who we have been both as individuals and as a people. We add to memory as we gain experience and insight; we adjust our memories in light of those same experiences and insight. Loss of memory is loss of identity.

Violence attempts to adjust our memories in a radical fashion in order to conform to the narrative of the lie. Any attempts to go back to our previous memory are met with threats of more violence. The experience of being stripped of our own narrative and the exposure of our vulnerability are such that many people will at a certain point embrace the lie because the pain and suffering of living without a narrative are too great.

The reconstruction of memory, however, is not simply a retrieval of memory. That old memory becomes so associated with violence that it becomes too painful to evoke. What must be done to overcome this suffering is to disengage the older memory from those acts of violence. That is done by repeating the narrative of the violence over and over again to ease the burden of trauma that it carries. Such an activity begins to put a boundary around the violence, as it were, to separate it from memory.

The tentacles of the lie burrow deep into memory, however, and extracting them does damage to the weave of memory. For that reason memory must be reconstructed.

It will never be quite the same; it will bear the scars of its history. But it can be so reconstructed.

Christianity, as all the great religious traditions, addresses the question of how to suffer and how to regain our humanity. It offers a larger narrative to which we might connect our own, and it offers a memory that can serve as the framework to rebuild the shattered one we have. It is to that story that we now turn.

3

The Christian Message
of Reconciliation

In the previous chapter we began an exploration of what may be the most problematic dimension of the reconciliation process in a shifting social order, that is, overcoming the suffering caused by violence as the first step in the process of reconciliation. Our path of investigation was to see violence not as antirational but as a counterrationality that strikes at the senses of safety and selfhood. This counterrationality constructs a narrative of the lie to counteract the narrative of truth that symbolizes the sense of safety and sense of self. To overcome the suffering caused by violence, one must not give into the lie and one must find some larger, redeeming narrative to restore truth.

In this chapter we turn to the theme of reconciliation itself, and particularly to the Christian definition of it. This is intended to help us answer the question about what resources Christians can offer in the rebuilding of societies ravaged by violence. We will begin by looking at the biblical resources for defining reconciliation, especially the Pauline and Deuteropauline materials. Thereafter we will take the findings from these resources and see how they give configuration to the reconciliation process, how they define and shape this difficult and necessary task.

RECONCILIATION IN THE PAULINE WRITINGS

The term *reconciliation* is not used that frequently in the scriptures. Indeed, it could not be considered a major preoccupation in the Bible. It is not used at all in the Hebrew Scriptures, although it is certainly implied in the concept of atonement.[6] Paul is the principal resource in the Bible for the concept of reconciliation. Some form of "to reconcile," *katallassein*, occurs just thirteen times in the authentic and Deuteropauline writings. Cilliers Breytenbach has argued recently that the usages in the authentic Pauline passages in Romans 5 and 2 Corinthians 5 are not connected with the older biblical ideas of atonement, but reflect a more secular usage, namely, a making of peace after a time of war.[7] Combining the references in Romans and 2 Corinthians with the usages in Colossians and Ephesians, José Comblin has suggested that a theology of reconciliation can be discerned on three levels: a christological level, in which Christ is the mediator through whom God reconciles the world to God's self; an ecclesiological level, in which Christ reconciles Jew and Gentile; and a cosmic level, in which Christ reconciles all the powers in heaven and on earth.[8] Let us explore each of these levels.

God Reconciling through Christ

Reconciliation with God does not occur in the same fashion as reconciliation among human beings. Paul is very clear in Romans and again in 2 Corinthians that reconciliation is the work of God. It is God who reconciles us to God's self; it is not a human work.

For if while we were enemies, we were reconciled to God through the death of his Son, much more surely, having been reconciled, will we be saved by his life. But more than that, we even boast in God through our Lord Jesus Christ, through whom we have now received reconciliation (Rom. 5:10-11).

All this is from God, who reconciled us to himself through Christ, and has given us the ministry of reconciliation; that is, in Christ God was reconciling the world to himself, not counting their trespasses against them, and entrusting the message of reconciliation to us (2 Cor. 5:18-19).

Paul takes the imagery connected with the usage of the term in his time, of enmity and friendship, to explain our relation to God. Again, it is important to note that it is God who initiates and carries through the reconciliation, and this is done by the death of Christ.

This all is, of course, familiar language. But it opens up a series of important ideas for our discussions of reconciliation here.

First and foremost, the reconciliation that Christians have to offer in overcoming the enmity created by suffering is not something they find in themselves, but something they recognize as coming from God. Thus the question is not *How can I bring myself, as victim, to forgive those who have violated me and my society?* It is, rather, *How can I discover the mercy of God welling up in my own life, and where does that lead me?* Reconciliation, then, is not a process that we initiate or achieve. We discover it already active in God through Christ.

It is this understanding of God taking the lead in the process of reconciliation that can confirm or give support to what was seen in the previous chapter; namely, the reconciliation process begins with the victim. Here the victim draws strength from experiencing the mercy and love of God. That gives the victim the courage to reach out in trust again, to overcome the ravages of the narrative of the lie. As it is put in 1 John "In this is love, not that we loved God but that he loved us" (1 John 4:10).

Second, God should not be seen as a source of indifferent mercy in this act of reconciling. The verses immediately preceding the Romans passage quoted above make that clear: "But God proves his love for us in that while we still were sinners Christ died for us. Much more surely then, now that we have been justified by his blood, will we be saved through him from the wrath of God" (Rom. 5:8-9). Here our sin causes God to be wrathful. Thus the offer of reconciliation is not given gratuitously, but comes to us from a God who has felt the enmity deeply, to the point of wrath. This is an important matter to ponder, inasmuch as wrath or anger is a significant but painful moment in overcoming the suffering caused by violence. It was spoken of in the previous chapter as "crying out." We often fear acknowledging or expressing anger against violence done to us. Our anger had to be suppressed when the violence was inflicted, lest it provoke even greater violence from the perpetrator. And there seems often to be a lingering sense that we may not acknowledge and express that anger after the fact, either because we still fear the reprisals of the assailant or because it seems to be countering violence with more violence. Anger can be destructive, but we also know that anger is an acknowledgment of the depth of pain and the breadth of the threat that has been made to our well-being. Not to express anger that arises from violence is not to acknowledge the suffering. And unless we do acknowledge it, a new narrative cannot be constructed.

An important corollary flows from this insight that God takes the initiative, that reconciliation is something that we discover rather than achieve. This insight reverses a

moment in the process of reconciliation that we usually
expect. We expect that evildoers should repent and so seek
forgiveness, that those who have wreaked terror and
oppression on a society should see the wrongness of their
ways and engage in repentance and reparation. However, *backwards*
in the Christian understanding of reconciliation, it works
the other way around. We discover and experience God's
forgiveness of our trespasses, and this prompts us to
repentance. In the reconciliation process, then, because
the victim has been brought by God's reconciling grace to
forgive the tormentor, the tormentor is prompted to
repent of evildoing and to engage in rebuilding his or her
own humanity. This is an important feature that is often
overlooked.

This point deserves some further elaboration. In the
reconciliation process as understood from such a perspective, the process is initiated by the victim, not the oppressor. This is not to place blame on the victim, as is often
done in cases of violence—that somehow the victims
deserve the violence that comes upon them. Rather, it calls
attention to the proper subjects and objects of reconciliation. The proper subject of reconciliation is the victim, not
the oppressor. And that can only be understood if we realize that the object of reconciliation is not the violent deed
done, but the humanity of the deed's perpetrator. We saw
in the previous chapter that what makes the suffering
coming from violence so difficult is that it tends to rob us
of our humanity. The victim is threatened in the act of
violence, and engaging in an act of violence robs the perpetrator of some measure of humanity. How else can one
murder or torture another human being? The victim
rediscovers his or her own humanity in trusting again, in
accepting in faith God's offer of humanity—the ability to
trust on a fundamental level. It is out of this welling up
of God's grace in the victim's shattered life that humanity
can be offered to the perpetrators of violence. For there

to be reconciliation, the victims must forgive; the perpe-trators cannot forgive themselves. And that forgiveness must carry something of the unboundedness of grace that God gives. We must not "count trespasses" any more than God has.

Anyone who has ever experienced violence knows how difficult that can be. But precisely herein lies the point: to undo the violence that has been done, only this kind of forgiveness can bring the perpetrator to repentance. Those who commit violence can be punished, but punish-ment does not guarantee repentance. Punishment can ful-fill a need for redress or vindication, but does it restore the humanity of the evildoer? Incarceration has been used as a form of punishment since the eighteenth century in many parts of the world not so much as a restraint but to provide a monastic-like setting to allow the prisoners to meditate on their sins and come to repentance. To that end prisons were designed to resemble monasteries (cells, horaria, uniform clothing, etc.). But as we know, such repentance is at best a hope and cannot be delivered by the penal system. The quality of forgiveness needed to effect true reconciliation requires a far more capacious source.

But let us return to the reflections on the Pauline pas-sages, namely, to a third point that can be derived from them. These passages present the means of reconciliation in Christ. Those means are both stark and striking: death, cross, blood. These three open up for us additional insights into reconciliation.

They show us, first of all, that the efforts needed to bring about reconciliation take us to the limits of human existence. They bring us to death, to violent death, to the relinquishing of the very source of life. Only an enmity that brings us to the utter limits of possibility could dare elicit such a strong means of reconciliation.

Second, these means—death, cross, blood—take us deep

into the epicenter of violence itself. Death on the cross was an insidious form of torture. It not only created wracking physical pain, it also provoked assaults on the dignity of the one crucified. The biblical passages about the passers-by taunting Jesus on the cross are indicative of this particular form of violence and humiliation (Luke 23:35-37). That blood would be shed, that substance sacred unto God and the source of God's life in humans, was understood as blasphemy and outrage. Thus the means of reconciliation not only take us to the limits of human existence, they take us into the very maw of violence. Christ's descent among the dead presents another image of going to the limits, but one that shows more the consequences of violence rather than the encounter with violence directly. The shedding of blood on the cross unto death confronts squarely the reality and the pervasiveness of violence. Thus this means of reconciliation becomes significant and perhaps even necessary to achieve that liberation from the suffering that accompanies violence.

That brings us also to a third dimension of the means of reconciliation in Christ. Blood is a paradoxical metaphor in the Hebrew Scriptures. It is a symbol of both life and death. And Paul develops in his writings the paradoxical nature of the cross as symbol as well: "For the message about the cross is foolishness to those who are perishing, but to us who are being saved it is the power of God" (1 Cor. 1:18). The cross is clearly a sign of death to most people, but it has become a sign of life to those who believe that Christ has passed from death on the cross to the resurrection: "I want to know Christ and the power of his resurrection and the sharing of his sufferings by becoming like him in his death" (Phil. 3:10). The paradoxical character of the symbols helps mediate the move from death to life in the reconciliation process. The symbols make possible the foursquare acknowledgment of violence, suffering, and death, but also provide the means for overcoming them. They do not escape the confrontation with violence, and they do not become hopelessly mired in it. They provide a vehicle for overcoming and transcending suffering, preparing the basis for reconciliation.

That brings us to a fourth consideration on the means of reconciliation in Christ. It is telling that Paul uses death, cross, and blood to express the means of God's reconciliation in Christ. All three, as has been noted, are very powerful symbols. They are all capable of carrying with them a thick network of meanings, meanings that may seem in themselves contrary or even contradictory to one another but are still held together by these symbols. It seems that nothing less than such symbols are necessary to help us reach reconciliation. We are not saved by univocal concepts, but through symbols that invite us to participation in their meanings. To be delivered from our sufferings we need something strong, something complex, something able to hold the contradictions of the situation together. Suffering from violence is acute not only because of the assault it makes on safety and selfhood, but because of the way it plays on our other unresolved vulnerabilities.

Those who work with victims of torture say that people with a strong sense of commitment have the best chances of recovering psychically and spiritually from the effects of torture. Those who do not hold strong beliefs or are accidental victims of torture have the least chance for recovery. One such tragic case of the latter will illustrate this point. Some years ago a young Haitian man I knew was arrested shortly after he returned to Haiti, mistaken for an activist against the Duvalier regime. He was held for several days and was beaten repeatedly before the mistake was discovered and he was released. He apparently recovered from the blows physically, but was unable to psychically. He lapsed into a deep depression and died six weeks later.

There is a corollary that can be derived from the power

and the paradox of the symbols of death, cross, and blood as mediating reconciliation. Reflection upon these three symbols cannot leave us harboring a consensus view of reality as the means to reconciliation. Somehow the conflict has to be faced. Somehow the violence has to be met on its own ground if it is to be overcome. And that requires a view of reality that includes conflict, albeit a conflict that will be overcome eschatologically.

A final comment: The reflections here on the meaning of God reconciling sinners to God's self did not venture into the area most commonly trod by theologians in the Latin church, namely, a discussion of satisfaction of God's honor. Such a discussion may be useful for describing the conclusions of the reconciliation process, in that the victim has received satisfaction for the violence perpetrated. The senses of honor and the legal metaphors that a discussion of satisfaction connotes may also be particularly useful in societies where shame and honor are powerful categories and where the rule of law has not been observed. I avoid moving into that track, however, since it has tended to blind Western theologians to other aspects of Paul's understanding of reconciliation that have been developed here, particularly the symbolic value of his reflections. We should remember, too, that the Greek church developed this strand of tradition differently; it emphasized metaphors of medicine and healing rather than legal metaphors. These metaphors may be more useful in organizing our understanding of deliverance from suffering and reconciliation in situations of violence and torture.[9] Moreover, too much preoccupation with the understanding of reconciliation as satisfaction can lead to seeing reconciliation in terms of technical rationality, a view from which the West has not totally escaped. Finally, a preoccupation with satisfaction may lead us away from a proper understanding of forgiveness into a kind of quid pro quo balancing.

These brief passages from Romans and 2 Corinthians open up for us a wonder-filled world that spans the depths of human terror and the liberating experience of deliverance from suffering into reconciliation. To complete this investigation of the biblical understandings of reconciliation, we need to turn now to the other two levels.

Reconciling Jew and Gentile

A preoccupation of Paul and his communities was the relation of Gentile and Jew. The Jews, the chosen people of God, had been offered the saving message of Jesus, but most had chosen to reject that message. Paul felt keenly his mission to the Gentiles, and so he had to settle in his mind how the chosen people could reject God's messenger, and how God could create a new chosen people from the Gentiles. Those people most clearly friends of God, it appeared, had become enemies of God, and those at greatest enmity had been reconciled to God.

The most famous locus for this struggle is, of course, Romans 9−11, where Paul, after much deliberation, declares the conversion of the Jews to Christ as only an eschatological event brought about by God. It reaches beyond his ability to fathom in any other fashion.

But apart from accounting for how God reconciles Jew and Gentile, how God reconciles past and present covenants, the Pauline literature reflects another approach in which the relative priority of Jew or Gentile is not the concern, but rather how God is making one people out of Jew and Gentile. This is clear in Ephesians and Colossians which, while likely not of Pauline authorship, still bear the imprint of his theology:

Remember that you were at that time without Christ, being aliens from the commonwealth of Israel, and strangers to the covenants of promise, having no hope and without God in the world. But now in Christ Jesus you who once were far off have been brought near by the blood of Christ. For he is our peace; in his flesh he has made both groups into one and has broken down the dividing wall, that is, the hostility between us. He has abolished the law with its commandments and ordinances, that he might create in himself one new humanity in place of the two, thus making peace, and might reconcile both groups to God in one body through the cross, thus putting to death that hostility through it (Eph. 2:12-16).

And you who were once estranged and hostile in mind, doing evil deeds, he has now reconciled in his fleshly body through death, so as to present you holy and blameless and irreproachable before him (Col. 1:22-23).

What insights might be derived from these passages? A general, recurring theme is suggested by Paul's reflection in Romans 9 – 11. Seeing God leading the Jews to Christ at the end of time reinforces God's reconciling role. But it also reminds us that the gigantic task of reconciliation in societies that have suffered violence and oppression is of nearly eschatological proportions.

The passages from Ephesians and Colossians just cited take up Paul's theme of God reconciling us to God's self, but offer along with that familiar theology a number of other dimensions that contribute to a Christian theology of reconciliation.

First of all, by focusing on the relations between Gentile and Jew and their mutual alienation from God, we see in sinner and sinned against, and in two peoples pitted against each other, something of the relationship between oppressed and oppressor in contemporary situations of violence. One must of course be careful not to find too exact a parallel, but the relations are suggestive.

Thus, alongside the image of our being enemies of God, the author of Ephesians suggests that in our unreconciled state we are aliens and strangers. This raises several interesting points worth pursuing here. The images of alien and stranger remind us of one of the principal ways human beings choose to draw boundaries that secure their safety and identity. They do this largely by exclusion, placing beyond that boundary those who are "not us," who are "them." These are the aliens and the strangers. These are the ones made "other."

The literature on the other and on the stranger is already large and continues to burgeon.[10] I wish to focus here on only a few points. In situations of violence it seems that both victim and assailant have to see each other as other, as the stranger. Otherwise no relation is possible. For the victim, it is inconceivable that the assailant could do such things to another human being. For the assailant, the victim has to be depersonalized in order to be violated. But more important is the question of the nature of that otherness. Seven ways of perceiving the other can be distinguished.

(1) We can *demonize* the other, treating the other as someone to be feared and eliminated if possible. In this way of perceiving, the other is seen as powerful and dangerous, possibly capable of overcoming us by sheer physical force. We can see this in the anticommunist stance taken by right-wing dictators as an excuse to perpetrate violence upon the population.

(2) We can, on the other hand, *romanticize* the other, treating the other as far superior to ourselves. The other becomes beyond our capacity to emulate, and underscores our degradation and deficiency. Vanquished peoples sometimes assume this posture.

(3) We can *colonize* the other, treating the other as infe-

rior, worthy of pity or contempt. In situations of violence, this is one of the attitudes commonly taken by oppressors, since it justifies their violence. The assumption is that the victims are not on the same level of humanity as the oppressor.

(4) We can *generalize* the other, treating the other as non-individual and thus bereft of personal identity. This happened in the case of the "disappearances" in Argentina, Chile, and other Latin American countries. The "disappeared" became non-persons.

(5) We can *trivialize* the other by ignoring what makes the other disturbingly different. Given the conflictive nature of situations of violence, this option is rarely invoked, since this way of perceiving is more at home in consensus models of reality.

(6) We can *homogenize* the other by claiming that there really is no difference. This is most in evidence in situations where two opposing groups are joined together forcibly by the oppressor. Consider in this regard the situation of many ethnic peoples in the Soviet Union, such as the Armenians and the Azerbaijanis.

(7) We can *vaporize* the other (in the sense of using a ray gun in science fiction literature to annihilate our opponent) by refusing to acknowledge the presence of the other at all. This is often found in cases of racism, where the oppressed people's existence is not even acknowledged. The oppressed become "invisible."

Not all of these possibilities will come into play in the relation between oppressor and victim. Sometimes a combination will occur. Most frequently, demonization takes place, with each treating the other as someone to be feared and eliminated. The oppressor often colonizes the victim, seeing the victim as inferior and therefore not worthy of normal human treatment. A long-term relation of violence can make the victim romanticize the oppressor as too strong to be resisted.

The point of exploring the quality of otherness in the other is twofold. First of all, other-making seems to be a constitutive part of the situation calling out for reconciliation. Hence, we must try to identify how the other has been made "other" in order to overcome this form of alienation. Without breaking through this, the narrative of the lie continues. Second, in the moment of reconciliation, we may have to decide how the other will be viewed hereafter. Will the common ground that we share with the other be the principal ground for reconciliation (we forgive when we realize that we are more the same than different)? Or will we try to tread that more difficult path of not seeing the other as better or worse, more or less important than ourselves, but simply equal to us yet still irreducibly different? Seeing the sameness in the other may be the more important approach to coming to reconciliation, it would seem, since this would describe "being aliens and strangers no longer." But seeing a fundamental difference, and embracing it, may be called for as well. This might be the case in reconciliation among races in South Africa where race as an index of difference will perdure long after apartheid, and only by acknowledging difference can reconciliation take place. Not to acknowledge enduring difference is to allow it to return to one of the seven categories of other-making described above.

Another contribution may be found in the references in both the Ephesians and Colossians passages to Gentile and Jew being made one flesh in the body of Christ. The images of the cross and the blood of Christ are repeated here too, but the addition of the image of the body of Christ suggests some other possibilities.

It was noted in the second chapter that a network of symbols surrounds our physical environment and provides a way of defining identity and securing safety. One of the most fundamental symbols is the body, both the physical human body and the social body.[11] Bringing the two alienated groups of Jews and Gentiles together in one body signifies that these two groups now share a common space within a common boundary. Thus, the alienation has passed away.

But there is another dimension of being restored in Christ's body. In the situations of violence described in the first chapter, especially situations of torture and imprisonment, the body is assaulted directly and physically. The damage is done both to the tissues and bones that make up the body and to the symbolic character of the body. Damage to the symbolic character of the body may have no physical correlate yet nonetheless wreaks considerable psychic damage. Thus, stripping the body and exposing it to public gaze, or depriving people of clothing over a long period of time has a shaming effect, especially strong in cultures with codes of honor and shame and in patriarchal settings where women are so exposed to men. The abused body of Christ, both beaten and crucified, and then exposed on the cross, becomes the vehicle of reconciliation for those who have had their own bodies abused. Here a theology of the Eucharist, in which one both receives and is taken up into the body of Christ, takes on a new significance. This is a theme that will be explored further in the final chapter.

A final suggestion can be drawn from this reflection on Jew and Gentile. In the Ephesians passage cited above, the author speaks of making out of the two alienated groups "one new humanity" (v.15). This opens up a theme that will be explored in more detail in the next section on cosmic reconciliation, but should be signalled here. We often think of reconciliation as overcoming alienation for the sake of returning to a peace that is a sort of status quo ante. But Christian reconciliation never takes us back to where we were before. It is more than the removal of suffering for the victim and conversion for the oppressor.

Reconciliation takes us to a new place. As Paul puts it in
the passage in 2 Corinthians immediately preceding his
discussion of reconciliation: "So if anyone is in Christ,
there is a new creation: everything old has passed away;
see, everything is made new!" This is a hard thing to imag-
ine, and easily slips out of our awareness if we do not
attend to it. We are aware that the oppressor must come
to a new place; there must be a turning away from evil
ways; there must be repentance. But we often forget that
the victim will be in a new place as well. Victims do not
just rediscover their humanity; they discover their
humanity in a new way. Part of their new way of being
human is the astonishing care that victims can provide for
their own oppressors, their uncanny ability to help not
only other victims, but also their oppressors discover their
humanity. This is an element to which we will return in
the discussion of the ministry of reconciliation in the final
chapter.

Again, these few passages from Ephesians and Colossians have shown themselves to be extremely rich in filling
out for us an understanding of reconciliation. We turn
now to the third level in our texts, that of cosmic reconciliation.

All Things Reconciled in Christ

The Pauline and Deuteropauline texts reveal another
dimension in which the reconciling activity of Christ is
seen. In Romans 11:15 Paul notes that the rejection of the
Jews has led to the reconciliation of the world: "For if
their rejection is the reconciliation of the world, what will
their acceptance be but life from the dead!" "World" here
would seem to mean the peoples of the world, counter-
posed to the Jews.

Colossians 1:19-20 goes much further in its depiction
of reconciliation: "For in him all the fullness of God was

pleased to dwell, and through him God was pleased to reconcile to himself all things, whether on earth or in heaven, by making peace through the blood of his cross." There is a parallel in the opening hymn in Ephesians where God "has made known to us the mystery of his will, according to his good pleasure that he set forth in Christ, as a plan for the fullness of time, to gather up all things in him, things in heaven and things on earth" (Eph. 1:9-10). In these two passages, "all things," *ta panta*, are gathered up in Christ, all things in heaven and on earth. This is certainly a more sweeping vision than the one found in Romans 11:15. But what does this kind of reconciliation mean?

The location of this reconciliation of all things in heaven and on earth in Ephesians and Colossians has led some to speculate that this reflects either Jewish or more likely Hellenistic cosmologies. At the very least, for Jewish believers, the heavens were filled with angels and the earth was stalked by demons. The Hellenistic worldview saw the earth surrounded by layer upon layer of spirits. This seems to be evident in the worldview of Colossians and also in the Letter to the Hebrews. Reconciliation then means the end of enmity between angels and demons for Jews and the overcoming of the alienating powers of the aeons in the Hellenistic worldview.[12] In the worldview of Asia Minor of that time, the aeons blocked access of the earth to God. They needed to be placated before supplicants could hope to pass to the next level. Colossians and Hebrews speak of Christ as having overcome the aeons and having given us direct access to God.

This particular worldview may seem especially ripe for demythologization in the minds of dominant culture North Americans. After all, we live in a universe but sparsely populated by spirits. Other contemporary cultures, of course, would not agree with us. Some of them see the world filled with spirits: some localized on the earth, others of varying power controlling different dimensions of terrestrial life and beyond.

This is not the place to make a case for or against the spirit world. There is, however, something that should be said regarding reconciliation on a cosmic level in the situations of violence and conflict that we have been exploring here. As was noted a little earlier in the discussion of God's reconciliation with the Jewish people, the sheer enormity of the challenge to reconciliation in some situations makes us look to a more cosmic solution. It seems that sometimes only a God can save us. To follow out all the places where the tentacles of evil have burrowed in a society seems to push us beyond any hope of eradicating the alienation in a situation. Moreover, no situation of violence and oppression stands completely in opposition to its past. Present alienation and evil feed on unresolved conflicts running back into the past and upon weaknesses and vulnerabilities borne from earlier experiences of oppression, violence, and failure. There is an enormous yet elusive character of wrongfulness that pervades a situation crying out for reconciliation, a character that cannot be clearly grasped or crisply defined. One of the things that happens in the process is that erstwhile clear boundaries become blurred and confused.[13]

In such situations, imagining these imponderables as aeons brooding over the world makes some sense. It reminds us in yet another way that the process of reconciliation is not reducible to a technical rationality in which everything can be circumscribed into definable tasks. Indeed, even larger or broader strategies seem unsuited to the enormity of the task. To enter into a process of reconciliation is better described as entering a *mysterion*, a pathway in which God leads us out of suffering and alienation into the experience of the grace of reconciliation. This grace is transforming, and creates the conditions of possibility not only for our forgiving our enemies, but also helping them rediscover their humanity. It was said earlier that reconciliation is not something achieved, but rather something discovered. Looking at reconciliation from this cosmic perspective may help illuminate that statement. Reconciliation is indeed the work of God, to which we are invited. We enter into that work and discover in a new way our own humanity. We come out of the process, like those in the mysteries, transformed—a new creation. In this we see how we do indeed come out in a new place.

A CHRISTIAN UNDERSTANDING
OF RECONCILIATION

Having explored these New Testament texts regarding reconciliation, what can be said to be the Christian understanding of this phenomenon? Let me summarize this in five points:

1. *It is God who initiates and brings about reconciliation.* We are not in a position, either as victims or oppressors, to create new narratives of sufficient power to overcome completely the damage that has been done by situations of violence and oppression. While we may overcome these situations, we seem never to be liberated completely; a residue of that violence and oppression has seeped into our bones. The structures we build to replace those from which we were liberated never quite get it right. One only need look to the struggles of Eastern Europe at this time to see this. This is not intended to encourage fatalism or quietism; we are indeed invited to cooperate in the process of reconciliation. But we must not forget whence it comes and who continues to guide it.

Since it was clear already in the last chapter that the victim is the one who begins the process of reconciliation, the victim is called upon to turn to God and experience God's reconciling grace, and so, himself or herself, to become the agent of reconciliation.

2. *Reconciliation is more a spirituality than a strategy.* One can define tasks and measure outcomes in a process of reconciliation. But the process cannot be reduced to a technical, problem-solving rationality. What undergirds a successful process of reconciliation is a spirituality, a view of the world that recognizes and responds to God's reconciling action in that world. That is why reconciliation is largely discovered rather than achieved. We experience God's justifying and reconciling activity in our own lives and in our own communities, and it is from that experience that we are able to go forth in a ministry of reconciliation. Thus, reconciliation becomes a way of life, not just a set of discrete tasks to be performed and completed. A reconciled person and a reconciled community live differently from the way they did before they encountered violence and oppression. Moreover, that ministry of reconciliation becomes a vocation, a continuing call to enter into reconciling activity.

An important corollary of discovering rather than achieving reconciliation is an awareness that forgiveness precedes repentance. We are prone to see repentance as proof of sincerity for seeking forgiveness—it is earning forgiveness. But the graciousness of God discovered in reconciliation also makes us aware that forgiveness is not something to be earned. It is given freely out of that same graciousness. That is why victims cannot be expected to forgive on a cue from someone else. Forgiveness dawns instead as a realization that it has already taken place.

3. *Reconciliation makes of both victim and oppressor a new creation.* Reconciliation is about more than righting wrongs and repenting of evildoing. These are surely included, but the understanding of reconciliation in the Christian Scriptures sees that we are indeed taken to a new place, a new creation. Reconciliation is not just restoration. It brings us to a place where we have not been before.

This is important to remember, because often in the early stages of the reconciliation process participants will have a too clear idea of what the outcome of reconciliation ought to be. Often how the oppressor will change is clearly imagined, with little reflection on the transformation of the victim. Both are brought to a new place; both are called into a new creation.

4. *The new narrative that overcomes the narrative of the lie is the story of the passion, death, and resurrection of Jesus Christ.* God works reconciliation through the death of God's son, Jesus Christ. This is not to be understood as an act of partriarchal sadism, but rather as an act of deep solidarity with suffering humanity, in which only by going into the maw of suffering, violence, and death can these be overcome. Body, blood, and cross are the symbols that appear over and over again in that narrative, symbols that can bear the paradox that is at the nucleus of the transformation of suffering and death into deliverance and life. The violence of our situations is met with the violence of Jesus' death; the dawning of the resurrection heralds that "new place" in which those reconciled hope to find themselves. The symbol of the body is the vehicle for restoring the shattered bodies of those who suffer and for gathering the scattered community of those driven apart in the situation of violence and oppression. The symbol of blood carries the memories of violence to be healed and portends new life for those who have shed their own blood. The cross reveals the lie of the oppressors' narrative. The cross challenges the understandings of what constitutes power in this world. God reveals power where the powerful of this world least expect it. That is most evident in reconciliation itself, where those who are weak, broken, and oppressed show the way to those who had wielded power.

5. *Reconciliation is a multidimensional reality.* Reconciliation involves not just God's reconciling activity. It

involves coming to terms with the otherness and the alienation that situations of violence and oppression have created. It involves lament and the healing of memory. It has an elusive cosmic dimension that we only dimly understand, but one which cannot be avoided in the quest for reconciliation. For it represents both those difficult to define qualities that go beyond a problem-solving approach to reconciliation and reminds us that reconciliation requires embracing all dimensions of reality.

This, put rather succinctly, seems to summarize major Christian insights into the process of reconciliation. It is these that form the background to the ministry of reconciliation, a ministry in which Paul exults so exuberantly in 2 Corinthians 5:20. That ministry of reconciliation will form the topic for the final chapter and provide the opportunity to bring together what has been explored here thus far.

4

The Church and the Ministry
of Reconciliation

The previous chapter focused upon the Pauline teaching on reconciliation and the implications that might be drawn from that narrow but rich lode for meeting the needs of situations calling out for reconciliation today. In exploring the biblical texts we noted Paul's enthusiastic words in 2 Corinthians:

> All this is from God, who reconciled us to himself through Christ, and has given us the ministry of reconciliation; that is, in Christ God was reconciling the world to himself, not counting their trespasses against them, and entrusting the message of reconciliation to us. So we are ambassadors for Christ, since God is making his appeal through us; we entreat you on behalf of Christ, be reconciled to God (2 Cor. 5:19-20).

These are strong and bold words on Paul's part, to insist that God is speaking through him, that he is an ambassador on behalf of Christ. Churches have continued since the time of Paul to take upon themselves the mantle of reconciliation, calling warring parties to peace, working toward the end of alienation, pulling down the walls of hostility.

Two questions immediately arise in reflecting upon the ministry of reconciliation: Under what conditions may the church assume the ministry of reconciliation? What does the ministry of reconciliation entail? It is these two questions that will occupy our attention in this final chapter. They help make concrete much of what has been said in the previous chapters. And they bring us into confrontation with the difficult situations where reconciliation must take place.

CAN THE CHURCH BE A MINISTER
OF RECONCILIATION?

We cannot begin our investigation of the church's role in the ministry of reconciliation without raising the question: Under what circumstances may the church exercise such a ministry? Some may presume that the church has an absolute right to do this, but unfortunately experience dictates otherwise.

By its intimate bond with its Master, and as a mediator of God's grace, the church may well have an abstract right to the ministry of reconciliation, but the church may historically forfeit that right in circumstances where it has been part of the problem. And it must be admitted that all too often the church itself has been on the side of the oppressor in situations that afterward cry out for reconciliation.

The authors of the *Kairos Document* in 1985 identified what they called "church theology" in the situation of crisis in South Africa. "Church theology," as the authors analyzed it, took the concepts of reconciliation, nonviolence, and justice and watered them down to make them palatable to the ruling powers supporting apartheid. *Reconciliation* came to mean negotiation in an atmosphere that gave legitimacy to the claims of both sides. But what kind of legitimacy can the evil of apartheid claim? Such a call for reconciliation, for working out of differences, ignores the prior call for justice. And as we saw in the first chapter, there can be no reconciliation without justice. Reconciliation without justice is a mere papering over of differences. It only leads to new outbreaks of violence and oppression. It is an attempt to establish peace and unity without truth, and for that reason is bound to fail.[14]

The *Kairos Document* also faults church theology's understanding of justice, which it characterizes as a justice of reform, a justice whose terms are set by the white oppressor as a kind of concession to the oppressed. These terms usually call for individual conversions and leave the sinful and oppressive structures untouched. It is a call for justice from the top down and ignores the cries of the poor.

Likewise, church theology's decrying violence limits itself only to certain kinds of violence, usually the violence that grows out of the frustration of the oppressed. What is not decried is the violence of the oppressor, which may not have the same overt physical character, but has equally devastating effects. Calls for nonviolence often do not take these more subtle but still deadly kinds of violence into account.[15]

What is lacking in this church theology? Social analysis, a political strategy, and an appropriate faith and spirituality that deals with this-worldly realities, these authors tell us. The *Kairos Document*'s nuanced but firm analysis may not apply to the churches in every country. Some churches, for example, have done far less about injustice than have the churches of South Africa. The image of the archbishop of Port-au-Prince fleeing for his life in January 1991 as a crowd of angry poor people set fire to the old

cathedral is a stark picture of the results of indifference
to the suffering of the oppressed.

Others have done more. Notable among the latter is the
Roman Catholic Church in Chile, by far the largest religious body there. Raul Cardinal Silva made his opposition
to the Pinochet government clear from the very beginning
in 1973. The Archdiocese of Santiago set up within its
structures a Vicariate of Solidarity, which served both as
a documentation center and as an advocacy arm for those
whose relatives had "disappeared." As the bishops developed the theme of reconciliation in the mid-1980s, it was
written into their national pastoral plan as "reconciliation
in truth," that is, a reconciliation that did not forget the
past, did not elide over injustice, but one that would call
for the truth to be revealed as a condition for reconciliation. As the Pinochet regime came to an end, they established "houses of reconciliation" throughout the country
where victims of the regime could come to tell their story,
to struggle, as it were, to overcome the narrative of the
lie that had lain like a heavy pall over Chile for seventeen
years.

The church in Chile is an example of a church that has
earned its right to exercise a ministry of reconciliation. It
has stood by the people against the government throughout the struggle and now can be an agent of reconciliation,
an ambassador of the wounded and suffering Christ to a
people coming out of the nightmare of the Pinochet years.
Other churches could be cited as examples. One thinks of
the Roman Catholic Church in the Philippines in the
struggle against Ferdinand Marcos in 1986, or the Evan-
gelical Lutheran Church in East Germany and the
Reformed Church in Hungary and Roumania in 1989.

Most churches find themselves somewhere between the
courage of the church in Chile and the abject collaboration
of the church in Haiti, between the resoluteness of a Cardinal Silva and the cowardice of an Archbishop Ligonde.

Churches, for all their wrapping themselves in the mantle of the prophet, usually end up reflecting the tensions and divisions of the larger society, especially when the churches themselves are quite large and are coextensive with large segments of the population. To some extent, this comes as no surprise. Church leaders, who are concerned about preserving the unity of the church, are keenly aware of how damaging divisiveness is to the church as the body of Christ. While that concern for patient attention to all and to inclusion is important, it cannot be used as an excuse for trucking with the narrative of the lie. The church must stand for truth in its entirety and with all its uncomfortableness if it is to witness to the gospel of Jesus Christ.

Likewise, the church cannot assume automatically that it has a mediating role between victims and oppressors. Because the church mirrors society, it may find that the lines dividing society run right through the center of the church. We noted this in the first chapter, pointing out that some members of the church choose to collaborate with an oppressive regime in order to allow for some public activity on the part of the church. Others choose the path of resistance and utter opposition to the regime, paying for their stance with imprisonment, exile, and even death. Sometimes church leaders side with an oppressive government for the sake of "peace," while some of their local clergy and members choose opposition. The ministry of reconciliation is not just something that the church exercises; at times the church is in need of that ministry itself. Reconciliation within the church can be as necessary as reconciliation within the larger society.

It should not surprise us that this might be the case. Indeed, a church can regain some of its legitimacy by seeking reconciliation within itself as a model for what will be needed in the larger society. It may seek both reconciliation within itself and reconciliation with the victims in society that it did not choose to heed. It is rare that such things actually happen. Two of the few examples that come to mind in recent years are the apologies of the United Church of Canada to the native peoples of Canada in 1988, and the admissions of the failings of the Roman Catholic Church in Poland to the Jewish community in Poland in 1990.

So what are the conditions under which the church may assume the ministry of reconciliation? (The presumption here is that the oppressive structures have been dismantled, as is now the case in much of Eastern Europe, or in Chile. If that has not yet happened, the role of the church is clear in the reconciliation process at this stage—it must work for the abolition of those structures.) We have seen that the reconciliation process begins with the healing of victims by God's reconciling grace. They in turn work healing on the oppressors, offering the forgiveness that sparks repentance. If the victims invite the church into this process, it seems to me that the church needs to accept whatever role is meted out to it. The victims are God's little ones, the *anawim,* who have shared in the cross of Christ. If they accept the church in the role of reconciliation, the church has a role. If they do not, the church's attempts at reconciliation will be fruitless.

More likely than speaking about "the church" in reconciliation, however, is to speak of those small communities of the church where reconciliation will take place. These communities come about through members themselves experiencing reconciliation. Often new communities are formed around or from precisely those members. It is important to realize that reconciliation takes place on this scale. It will involve each person coming to experience reconciliation with God and rediscovery of his or her own humanity in that process. Out of that experience comes the call to a ministry of reconciliation.

Such communities may have to distance themselves for

a time from the larger church, especially if that church has been implicated in the very violence that now must be overcome. There may be a need to be a prophetic sign to the church, to call the church out of its sin and back to its Lord. But such separation cannot be a permanent thing. Were that so, the very ministry of reconciliation of those communities would be contradicted. The brokenness and upheaval that a society undergoes when its social order has changed may warrant such a move. It is better, if possible, that such communities maintain a certain separateness within the body of the church, keeping open at all times to the beginning of that narrative that will overcome the narrative of the lie.

If the church has a sense of its own sinfulness and a sense of its own limits, it will find its place in the process of reconciliation. In South African theologian John de Gruchy's phrase, the church must exercise "a prophetic ministry in a pastoral way."[16] To do this does not mean to engage in some symmetrical balancing act. The exigencies of prophecy never really allow for that, since justice and injustice are never represented in the world symmetrically or equally. Rather, what is called for is a ministry of truth and a pastoral initiative that recognizes the fact that all are sinners and in need of God's help and care. The balance is between the church's understanding of its own sinfulness and its recognition of the sinfulness of those to whom it reaches out. In this manner a way can be found into the ministry of reconciliation.

THE MINISTRY OF RECONCILIATION

All of this having been said, just what concrete forms does the ministry of reconciliation take? We explored some of the elements of a way to approach a history of violence and searched out some of the Christian contributions to a reconciliation process. How does this come about concretely in a ministry of reconciliation? In this final section, I would like to explore how all of these considerations might come together.

The result is not a tightly knit plan. After all, the assertion made repeatedly here is that reconciliation is something that comes upon the victim, something that the victim discovers, rather than something that is achieved by a well-managed therapy or process. It is more a spirituality than a strategy.

Moreover, different situations call for different configurations. The situations that I will be presuming in the remarks that follow are those where the oppressive regimes have fallen or are gone, where now a rebuilding must take place. In situations where that has not yet happened but seems likely to come about soon (say, for example, in South Africa), these remarks might be read as a preparation for that time, although the future is always different from what we expect it to be. For situations where the oppression is still very much in place, it is probably too early to talk of reconciliation on a wide-scale basis, although individuals may achieve the level of reconciliation needed in their own lives to begin such a ministry. The principal task in such situations is the continuing struggle against injustice.

I would like to divide these observations into two sections. The first will deal with the spirituality of reconciliation; that is, those attitudes that characterize the minister of reconciliation. The second will deal with some of the resources that the church can bring to bear in the ministry of reconciliation.

The Spirituality of Reconciliation

It was noted above that reconciliation was ultimately a spirituality and not a strategy. This was not said to take away the urgency or to blunt the prophetic edge of reconciliation; it was advanced, rather, to recognize some of its salient characteristics. It grew out of the realization that reconciliation is not something that we can manufacture for ourselves. It comes upon us like healing. The metaphor of healing, long beloved in the Orthodox church, is an apt one. Healing takes its own time. It requires that the patient attend to matters of health. So, too, it seems to me, with reconciliation. Let me suggest three characteristics that mark the spirituality of reconciliation.

The first is an attitude of listening and waiting. Victims of violence and suffering must tell their story over and over again in order to escape the narrative of the lie. As they recount their own narrative, little by little they begin to construct a new narrative of truth that can include the experiences of suffering and violence without allowing those experiences to overwhelm it. This includes, in the first stage, establishing a kind of geography of violence and suffering; that is, bounding it so as to tame its savage power. The more that the violence is so bounded, the less formidable it becomes. Without such boundedness, it roams at will in the life of the victim devouring, like the roaming lion in 1 Peter 5:8, whomever it will. The ministry of reconciliation at this stage is a ministry of listening. Those ministers who themselves have experienced reconciliation will make for the best listeners in this situation.

The other dimension of this first characteristic is closely allied to listening. It involves learning how to wait. North Americans, especially those from the dominant culture, are notoriously poor at waiting. Waiting is considered lost time, empty time that needs to be filled up with something. In an age where information is one of the greatest forms of wealth, "lost" time is seen as lost wealth, because time becomes one of the most important commodities in this kind of world. On the other hand, what the poor of the world have is a lot of time. They are always made to wait. They wait in line for social services, they wait to be hired, their time is not considered valuable like that of the wealthy.

More contemplative traditions teach us that waiting is an active capacity. It is in learning to wait that we come to discern the difference between living in illusion and living in reality.[17] Learning to wait involves being calm and comfortable with ourselves—something victims of violence and suffering must relearn. It also involves waiting on God and God's reconciling grace—an opportunity God takes to teach us all kinds of other things along the way. Learning to wait is important, because it takes time to allow painful memories to surface and be renarrated, for deep and penetrating wounds to heal, and for reconciliation to well up in our souls. The waiting is not just empty time that must be marked until things happen; it is part of the formative experience itself that moves us out of illusion—the narrative of the lie—into reality—the narrative of the truth.

The second characteristic of the spirituality of reconciliation is attention and compassion. Attention grows from learning to wait. Our attention spans have been made noticeably shorter by the electronic media. Attention must be restored if reconciliation is to take place. An inability to attend is often the result of torture, for example, since the pain of torture builds in the fear that staying too long in one place will bring back that pain. Lack of attention is an attempt to escape the current situation. Attention requires calm. Attention likewise is needed if all that has happened is to be faced. Just as any spirituality cannot hope to grow without turning its attention constantly to God, so too attention to the healing of painful memories is of the essence in the ministry of reconciliation.

Attention, in turn, is the basis of compassion, of an ability to wait and to be with, to walk alongside a victim at the victim's pace. The root of the word *compassion* is, of course, "to feel or suffer with." We can never entirely enter into another's suffering, although we can enter again our own suffering, which might parallel that of another. What we may lack in empathy or parallel experience we can make up in attention, an attention that does not impale the victim but creates an environment of trust and safety.

The third characteristic of the spirituality of reconciliation is its post-exilic stance. This terminology comes from South African theologian Charles Villa-Vicencio, who compares the post-apartheid situation in South Africa with Israel returning to Jerusalem after the Exile in Babylon. A new society has to be constructed on the ruins of the old society. The society will need a new law, but it will be a *deuteronomos*, a second law. The experience of exile will bring a new, chastened outlook to the returnees.

Villa-Vicencio's suggestion is a fruitful one, I think. Dwelling on the post-exilic biblical literature as a resource for living in a post-exilic time today can help sustain the spirituality of reconciliation. It can provide it with nourishment from the great prophets of the post-exilic time. Indeed, one of the images that I have employed here for the experience of reconciliation—of reconciliation welling up in the soul—is taken from the vision of water flowing from the temple in Ezekiel 47.

It was noted earlier that reconciliation is not just a task to be achieved. For those who are reconciled, reconciliation becomes a calling. They move to a wholly new place, from which they call oppressors to repentance and serve in a prophetic way for the whole of society. A spirituality that will sustain them is of utmost importance. The characteristics sketched out here—of listening and waiting, of attention and compassion, of living a post-exilic existence—all come together to support the reconciler in the ministry of reconciliation. We now turn to other resources.

The Church's Resources for Reconciliation

The church has a number of internal resources to aid
the ministry of reconciliation. I would like to point to a
number of them in this section.

The first is the power of ritual. Ritual is sometimes
downplayed in secular societies as neurotic repetition.
Feminists in these kinds of cultures have taken the lead
in helping their dominant culture rediscover the importance of ritual in touching parts of our lives and expressing
deeply felt but hardly articulated feelings. In dealing with
the stages of reconciliation, ritual becomes extremely
important, because the drama of ritual can speak of that
for which we have no words.

One example has been the opportunity to celebrate the
Eucharist in public again, as has been so evident in the
Soviet Union since 1990. Other rituals, however, are
directed more pointedly at the experience of suffering of
the past. Notable in Chile was a ritual of purification of
the National Stadium in Santiago. This was the holding
place for those first arrested in the roundups in Santiago
after the 1973 coup. Some nine hundred people were executed in the stadium; others disappeared from the stadium, never to be seen again. The purification was a way
of remembering those who had died there; it also provided
the opportunity to exorcise, in some measure, the horrors
that occurred there.

A closely related ritual is providing funerals and proper
burials for victims of the oppression. One of the first acts
of the free Hungarian Parliament was to disinter the
remains of Imre Nagy, the prime minister of Hungary
executed in the uprising in 1956 and buried in an
unmarked grave, and give him a state funeral. A friend of
mine recently presided at a funeral for the proper inter-
ment of the remains of eighteen people, members of a
workers' group, found in a mass grave about five hundred

kilometers south of Santiago. I asked him how the survivors responded. He said that all were quite calm. The one thing they wanted was a proper burial for their loved ones after seventeen years. One of the survivors was a mother who that day had the remains of two sons interred. A third son had committed suicide as a result of the disappearance of his two brothers. Her only daughter left the country to live in Colombia, because she could no longer abide all that had happened to the family. Her strategy for survival was escape. The mother is now alone. For her, the funeral meant that her two sons were now finally at rest. Her family was destroyed, but somehow she has found peace.

The church cannot underestimate the power of its rituals to mark the moments of transition in reconciliation, and to give expression to feelings so painful and so deep that no other way can be found to bear them. For Catholic and Orthodox traditions of Christianity, this turn to ritual may come easier than for Reformation traditions. But all will need to draw upon ritual according to their best lights.

For those traditions that celebrate penitential reconciliation sacramentally, that ritual becomes a vehicle to move beyond dealing with individual sin and embrace the patterns of public penitence that marked the early church. This may prove especially useful when the church itself finds that it has sinned and needs to repent. Ways need to be devised to capture once again the wealth of that sacrament for these kinds of situations.

One ritual needs to be singled out here, and that is the Eucharist. Eucharistic theologies and practices vary among the churches, but the need for deliverance from the suffering of violence may draw them together around those texts in Colossians and Ephesians discussed in the previous chapter. Gathering around the eucharistic table, the broken, damaged, and abused bodies of individual victims and the broken body of the church are taken up into the body of Christ. Christ's body has known torture; it has known shame. In his complete solidarity with victims, he has gone to the limits of violent death. And so his body becomes a holy medicine to heal those broken bodies of today. Partaking of the body and blood of the Lord is, as Paul reminds us in 1 Corinthians 10:16, partaking in the death of the Lord. Sharing the cup of the blood of the Lord unites us with the cup that he had to drink, a cup that gathers in the sufferings of the saints.

The need for reconciliation brings a new urgency to the celebration of the Eucharist. It recalls the dangerous memory of the passion and death of Christ, the narrative of truth that exposes the lie of violence. It is the story of the innocent one who suffers and dies, but whom death cannot hold. It means that those who are taken up into Christ's broken body are not forgotten. If we die with him, we will surely live with him.

Another resource that the church can draw upon is images from the New Testament. Images give examples of retelling the story, of shaping new narratives out of tragedy. One such image is in Luke 15:11-32, the parable of the prodigal and his brother. In the story the elder son complains to his father that "this son of yours [he does not call him "my brother"] came back, who has devoured your property with prostitutes, and you killed the fatted calf for him!" But the father corrects the narrative his elder son has recounted: "This brother of yours [note how the father reaffiliates him to his estranged brother] was dead and has come to life; he was lost and has been found." The father celebrates the return of the prodigal as the return from death to life. The son who lived with pigs has rediscovered his humanity and seeks reconciliation. In embracing his son, the father reshapes the narrative that his elder son had constructed.

A second image also comes from Luke, this time chapter 24:13-35. Here we have another example of reshaping the narrative. In this account two of Jesus' disciples are on the road to Emmaus "talking with each other about all these things that had happened." Jesus meets them and walks along with them, listening to their narrative. He asks them to explain, which they begin to do, ending with "but we had hoped that he was the one to redeem Israel." Jesus then counters with his own version of the narrative: " 'Was it not necessary that the Messiah should suffer these things and then enter into his glory?' Then beginning with Moses and all the prophets, he interpreted to them the things about himself in all the scriptures."

When Jesus leaves them, "they said to each other, 'Were not our hearts burning within us while he was talking to us on the road, while he was opening the scriptures to us?' " The account ends with them rushing back to Jerusalem to tell the other disciples "what had happened on the road." They continue, in effect, the new narrative.

Both of these accounts are splendid examples of reshaping narratives. Others could be pointed out, such as Jesus' verbal repartee with the Samaritan woman at the well (John 4:7-26). But all of these point to the tremendous power that narratives have to shape our identities and our lives. In the process of reconciliation, this healing of memories and reshaping of narratives is a process that can be enhanced by using the resources the scriptures give us.

A final image from the scriptures comes from John 20:19-29, when the risen Jesus appears to Thomas. There are two things worth singling out in this story. The first is the wounds of Jesus. Even though he has been transformed beyond death, Jesus still bears the wounds of his torture. Death has transformed much about Jesus, but his wounds still remain. One of the things that many who have been tortured or otherwise violated must bear is that they will be disabled in some ways for the rest of their lives. They are not cured of their wounds. Their wounds, in some way, will never heal. While this is a handicap for them — emotionally or physically — that handicap has been discovered by some to be a spiritual resource. The blind seer and the wounded healer are images known to us and are sometimes romanticized a bit. But there are such people, who, in their disablement from a violent past, find their calling to work as reconcilers. By their wounds we are healed.

Second, there is Thomas' confession of faith. This passage is often narrated to highlight his unbelief. But there is another reading of the text. In this, the frightened disciple Thomas rediscovers his Lord and God as he is invited to believe and to touch the wounds of Christ. These two — belief and touching the wounds — come together as invitation and as gift. They provoke in Thomas the moment of faith, that moment of trust in which he can rediscover his own humanity. By confessing Jesus as his Lord and God, Thomas experiences the overcoming of his fear and his distance from Jesus.

In the process of reconciliation we are called into faith and invited to touch the wounds of Christ. In that faith we rediscover our own humanity, expressed most poignantly in that reaching out in trust. By restoring trust we restore the ability to live in human society. In touching those wounds we encounter a God who has suffered with us and who continues to bear the marks of his torture even in his resurrection from the dead. The wounds betoken memory, but a memory woven into a new narrative of truth.

The final resource that the church has to offer is the cross. To make an instrument of torture the very emblem of its self-understanding as the bearer of God's good news is a bold act. The cross stands starkly on the landscape, at once instrument of torture and throne of God, as John's gospel so clearly depicts it. The cross sums up the paradox of our world and of the God who relates to that world. Our world is wracked by violence, but it can also bring forth incredible beauty. It strangles itself in narratives of the lie, but it can also draw out narratives of the truth. The cross stands in the midst of that world so that we might never forget the anguish of broken bodies and spirits, but also so that we might not lose hope. For it is through the cross that God has chosen to reconcile the world. In using the cross in that way God teaches us something fundamental about the nature of power. Human power is a very unstable thing, something that easily runs amok in violence. Divine power comes to us as service and solidarity: power as self-emptying, utterly trusting; power as deciding to stand firm with those who suffer when flight would seem to be the better strategy. It is only this kind of power that can prevail. It is the power of the stripped and tortured One on the cross, who has chosen not to come down from that cross, but to stay with the victims of violence even into the maws of death. This is the redeeming narrative that is offered to victims of violence. This is the kind of God who offers us reconciliation.

Conclusion

Much more could be said about reconciliation and the deliverance from suffering. We have tried to follow here but a few threads in this complex weave: the transformation of violence, the redeeming narrative, the biblical dynamics of reconciliation, the ministry of reconciliation in our own time amid shifting social contexts away from oppressive regimes to what are hoped to be more just societies. We are standing between the times, effectively at the end of what was called the twentieth century, awaiting the birth of a new reality. In the midst of that waiting the suffering from the violence of this century comes rushing toward us, calling out for reconciliation. It is a time, this time between the times, for confronting the lie and telling the truth. It is a time to learn to wait and watch, while others rush and rant. An exhilarating, exasperating time.

These reflections might best conclude with the words of two people who have experienced the violence of this century and have found the reconciliation of God welling up in their souls.

The first is from František Cardinal Tomášek, the Roman Catholic Primate of Czechoslovakia, who was ninety years old at the downfall of the Communist regime in 1989. He himself had suffered years of imprisonment and had led the church in Czechoslovakia fearlessly for over two decades. In his first public address to the people of Czechoslovakia after freedom came he said: "Let us fight for the good with good means! We have seen in our oppressors the short-lived victory of malevolence, of hatred, of revenge, of ruthlessness, of arrogance." Those are the words of someone who has tasted reconciliation.

The second are words from Mr. Joe Seramane, now director of the Justice and Reconciliation Department of the South Africa Council of Churches. His witness to justice led to imprisonment and torture. He tells us that "it is through reconciliation that we regain our humanity. To work for reconciliation is to live to show others what their humanity is." I hope that we can take his advice.

Notes

1. James H. Cone, *Black Theology and Black Power* (New York: Seabury, 1969), 143-52.

2. José Comblin, "O tema de reconciliação e a teologia na America Latina," *Revista Eclesiastica Brasileira* 46, no. 182 (1986), 272-314; in a slightly different form in *Reconciliación y liberación* (Santiago de Chile: CESOC, 1987), 9-65. For the *Kairos Document*, see "The *Kairos* Document: Challenge to the Church," *Journal of Theology for Southern Africa*, no. 53 (1985), 61-81.

3. John Carroll, "Socio-political Dimensions of Reconciliation," *East Asian Pastoral Review* 21 (1984), 213-25.

4. See especially, René Girard, *Violence and the Sacred* (Baltimore: The Johns Hopkins University Press, 1977; original publication, Paris: Ed. Bernard Grasset, 1972), and *The Scapegoat* (Baltimore: The Johns Hopkins University Press, 1986; original publication, Paris: Ed. Grasset & Faquelle, 1982).

5. The term *orthopathema* was introduced to me by Samuel Solivan, to whom I express my gratitude.

6. For a brief overview of the cognate usages in the Hebrew Scriptures, see Cilliers Breytenbach, "On Reconciliation: An Exegetical Response," *Journal of Theology for Southern Africa*, no. 70 (1990), 64-68.

7. Cilliers Breytenbach, *Versöhnung. Eine Studie zur paulinischen Soteriologie* (WMANT, 60; Neukirchen-Vluyn: Neukirchener Verlag, 1989).

8. Comblin, 276-94. I follow Comblin in his exegesis in the discussion that follows.

9. For a brief overview of Greek approaches to reconciliation, see Sergei Hackel, "Paths to Reconciliation: Some Ways and Byways from the Orthodox Past," *Epiphany* 6 (1986:4), 30-36.

10. For a general survey of the literature on the other, see Edward Farley, *Good and Evil: Interpreting a Human Condition* (Minneapolis: Fortress Press, 1990), 33 n.6.

11. Among the rich literature being developed on the body, especially in feminist circles, the pioneering work of anthropologist Mary Douglas, *Natural Symbols: Explorations in Cosmology* (New York: Vintage Paperbacks, 1973) should be singled out. See in that collection especially her essay "The Two Bodies."

12. I explore this further in *In Water and in Blood: A Spirituality of Solidarity and Hope* (New York: Crossroad, 1988), 110-13.

13. See, for example, the account of the Roman Catholic Church in Hungary by Imre Kozma, " 'Die Palme wächst unter der Last': Katholische Kirche in Ungarn," in *Katholische Kirche in Osteuropa Verfolgung, Freiheit und Wiedergeburt* (Königstein/T.: Kirche in Not/Ostpriesterhilfe, 1990), 75-84.

14. "The *Kairos* Document: Challenge to the Church," 3.1 (pp. 67-69). I would not agree, however, with their stance that repentance precedes forgiveness. Nor does James B. Torrance, "Listening to its Challenge," *Journal of Theology for Southern Africa*, no. 55 (1986), 42-45.

15. "The *Kairos* Document: Challenge to the Church," 3.2–3.3. (pp. 69-72). For a more adequate response of the church to violence and nonviolence see Ernesto Ranly, "Spiritualité et violence au Pérou," *Spiritus*, no. 121 (1990), 365-77.

16. John de Gruchy, "The Struggle for Justice and the Ministry of Reconciliation," *Journal of Theology for Southern Africa*, no. 62 (1988), 43-52.

17. For a close reading of this phenomenon as it applies to living in cross-cultural situations, see Lawrence J. Lewis, *The Formative Experience of Waiting: Moving from Living in Illusion to Living in Reality.* Ph.D. diss., Duquesne University, 1984.